TOP **10**
LISBON

TOMAS TRANÆUS

EYEWITNESS TRAVEL

Left **Castelo de São Jorge** Centre **Archeological finds, Sé Catedral** Right **Praia da Bela Vista**

LONDON, NEW YORK,
MELBOURNE, MUNICH AND DELHI
www.dk.com

Produced by Coppermill Books
55 Salop Road London E17 7HS

Reproduced by Colourscan, Singapore
Printed and bound in China by Leo

First American Edition, 2007
09 10 9 8 7 6 5 4 3 2 1

Published in the United States by
DK Publishing, 375 Hudson Street, New York,
New York 10014

Reprinted with revisions 2009

**Copyright 2007, 2009 ©
Dorling Kindersley Limited, London
A Penguin Company**

A catalog record for this book is available from the
Library of Congress.

ISSN 1479-344X
ISBN: 978-0-7566-4576-2

Within each Top 10 list in this book, no hierarchy of
quality or popularity is implied. All 10 are, in the editor's
opinion, of roughly equal merit.

Floors are referred to throughout in accordance with
British usage; ie the "first floor" is the floor
above ground level.

> **We're trying to be cleaner and greener:**
>
> • we recycle waste and switch things off
> • we use paper from responsibly managed
>   forests whenever possible
> • we ask our printers to actively reduce
>   water and energy consumption
> • we check out our suppliers' working
>   conditions – they never use child labour
>
> **Find out more about our values and
> best practices at www.dk.com**

Contents

Lisbon's Top 10

The information in this DK Eyewitness Top 10 Travel Guide is checked regularly.
Every effort has been made to ensure that this book is as up-to-date as possible at the time of
going to press. Some details, however, such as telephone numbers, opening hours, prices,
gallery hanging arrangements and travel information are liable to change. The publishers
cannot accept responsibility for any consequences arising from the use of this book, nor for
any material on third party websites, and cannot guarantee that any website address in this
book will be a suitable source of travel information. We value the views and suggestions of
our readers very highly. Please write to: Publisher, DK Eyewitness Travel Guides,
Dorling Kindersley, 80 Strand, London WC2R 0RL.

Cover: Front – DK IMAGES: Linda Whitwam bl. PHOTOLIBRARY: photononstop/Tibor Bognor main. Spine – DK
IMAGES: Linda Whitwam b. Back – DK IMAGES: Linda Whitwam tc, tl; Peter Wilson tr.

Left **Parque das Nações** Centre **Art Nouveau tiles, Rua dos Sapateiros** Right **Rua Augusta**

eft **Torre de Belém** Right **Ponte 25 de Abril**

LISBON'S
TOP 10

LISBON'S TOP 10

🔟 Lisbon Highlights

These days, fewer visitors approach Lisbon from the sea than once used to, but the wide turn many airliners make over the beach at Caparica – before crossing the river above the red suspension bridge and sweeping over the city's roofs to the airport – is a pretty good introduction too. Lisbon is a city of immediate charms, and of a deeper beauty that must be sought out. The light loves it, painting it in warm pink hues and bright blues. It is an old place, steeped in history, but not closed in on itself as it once was. Lisbon's youthful, modern side includes a nightlife which is among Europe's liveliest, latest and most diverse.

1 Castelo de São Jorge

Crowning the hill where Lisbon's original settlers lived, the city's medieval castle is a successful and evocative reconstruction. Best of all are the views from the esplanade *(see pp8–9)*.

2 Mosteiro dos Jerónimos

The Manueline is Portugal's own architectural style. Its beginnings, and some of its greatest expressions, can be seen in the glorious national monument that is the Jerónimos Monastery *(see pp10–11)*.

3 Sé Catedral

Lisbon's cathedral was built for the city's first bishop in the middle of the 12th century, just after the Christian reconquest. It is a fortress-like structure whose stone glows amber as the sun sets *(see pp12–13)*.

4 Museu Nacional de Arte Antiga

Housed in a grand 17th-century palace, Portugal's national gallery displays art that places Portugal in a historical context – as well as other treasures *(see pp14–15)*.

Preceding pages **Elevador da Bica**

Parque das Nações

5 Flanked by the Vasco da Gama Bridge, the site of Lisbon's sea-themed Expo 98 has been transformed into a dynamic leisure, business and residential area *(see pp16–17)*.

Torre de Belém

6 The boot-shaped defensive tower at Belém is one of Lisbon's emblems, but it is also one of the most perfect examples of the Manueline style, with proportions that please, rather than inspire awe *(see pp18–19)*.

Museu Nacional do Azulejo

7 This beautiful museum displays and explains the essential Portuguese decorative element – the tile. It also has some of the city's most stunning convent and church interiors *(see pp20–21)*.

Palácio de Queluz

8 A Rococo feast, ripe with culture and aspiration, this summer palace just outside Lisbon was for a brief period the royal family's permanent residence. It still exudes an air of fussily ordered pleasure *(see pp22–3)*.

Museu Calouste Gulbenkian

9 A museum of the highest international calibre, the Gulbenkian is a small, coolly pleasant universe of art history, where visitors can drift around oblivious of any other *(see pp24–5)*.

Sintra

10 Sintra is a powerful magnet for most visitors to Lisbon, but it is wise to do as Lord Byron did, and absorb the city first before moving on to Sintra – the better to appreciate the contrast *(see pp26–7)*.

Map labels: AVENIDA DA BELÉM · AVENIDA JOÃO XXI · AVENIDA DA REPÚBLICA · AV. 5 DE OUTUBRO · AV. ANTÓNIO AUGUSTO DE AGUIAR · Campo Pequeno · Rego · Estefânia · Cemiterio do Alto de São João · Saldanha · PRAÇA DUQUE DE SALDANHA · Parque Eduardo VII · PRAÇA MARQUÊS DE POMBAL · RUA JOAQUIM ANT. DE AGUIAR · Moreiras · AVENIDA ALMIRANTE REIS · Bairro Lopes · Anjos · Rato · Graça · RUA D. POLITÉCNICA · Mouraria · São Bento · Bairro Alto · Baixa · Alfama · Estrela · CALÇADA DA ESTRELA · Chiado · RUA DE DOM LUÍS I · AVENIDA 24 DE JULHO · PRAÇA DO COMÉRCIO · AV. INFANTE DOM HENRIQUE

800 —— yards ¬ 0 ¬ metres —— 800

Lisbon's Top 10

7

⭐10 Castelo de São Jorge

This hilltop castle is traditionally regarded as the site of Lisbon's founding settlement. Recent archeological finds dated to the 6th century BC support this theory, although the oldest castle remains are from the Moorish era. Portugal's first king, Afonso Henriques, captured the Moorish citadel in 1147 and his successors added the Alcáçovas palace, which remained the royal residence until 1511. Following centuries of neglect, the castle was imaginatively restored in 1938, providing Lisbon with one of its most attractive viewpoints.

Figure of St George

🎥 The west-facing esplanade is at its best in the late afternoon, with a low sun painting everything in warm hues. Early mornings here are shady, and can be chilly.

🍷 The outdoor bars at Chapitô or Bar das Imagens *(see p60 for both)* are good places to digest a visit to the castle.

• Porta de São Jorge, Rua do Chão da Feira
• Map G4
• 21 880 06 20
• Open 9am–9pm (6pm Nov–Feb) daily
• Adm €5 (concessions and family groups €1.50; under-10s and over-65s free)
• Torrre de Ulisses open 10am–5pm daily (11am–2:30pm in winter); Olisipónia open same hours as castle

Top 10 Features

1. Porta de São Jorge
2. Esplanade
3. Statue of Afonso Henriques
4. Olisipónia
5. Casa do Leão
6. Inner Battlements
7. Torre de Ulisses
8. Torre de São Lourenço
9. Gardens
10. Santa Cruz Neighbourhood

Porta de São Jorge
This grand gate gives onto the final steep climb up to the castle grounds. In a wall niche to the left is a figure of St George *(above left)*. His local connection may derive from English troops' role in the conquest of Moorish Lisbon.

Esplanade
The esplanade on top of the outer fortifications is one of the main rewards of a climb up to the castle. Dotted with archeological remains and shaded by pines, it follows the castle's western perimeter, offering views of the river and the lower city *(below)*.

Statue of Afonso Henriques
This bronze statue of Portugal's first king was added to the esplanade in 1947. It is a copy of a romantic 1887 work by Soares dos Reis (the original is in Guimarães).

Olisipónia
The only building remaining from the historic Alcáçovas palace contains a thoroughly modern multimedia exhibit. This provides a lively summary of Lisbon's history in several languages.

For more Lisbon viewing points See pp36–7

5 Casa do Leão
This restaurant, in one of Lisbon's most exclusive locations, serves classic Portuguese and international food. The interior was part of the 13th-century Alcáçovas palace, but sit outside if you can; the views are superb.

6 Inner Battlements
The reconstruction of the inner castle is one of the great achievements of the 1938 restoration. With ten towers and a dividing inner wall, the restored castle matches, as far as possible, the original's layout and size.

7 Torre de Ulisses
In one of the inner battlement towers, a camera obscura attached to a periscope projects images of the city. The castle has a history of distant gazing: Lisbon's first observatory was set up there in 1779.

8 Torre de São Lourenço
Connected to the castle by a long series of steps *(right)*, this tower once formed part of the outer fortifications. Today, it offers another angle from which to view the castle.

9 Gardens
Don't miss the peacocks in the shady castle gardens – and look out for the excavations of a Moorish village.

10 Santa Cruz Neighbourhood
The tiny and partially restored neighbourhood of Santa Cruz do Castelo (within the old citadel) is one of the most picturesque parts of Lisbon *(left)*. It is home to ageing residents as well as younger investors and luxury hotels.

Mythical martyr
The myth of Martim Moniz, a soldier who is said to have given his life as a doorstopper in 1147, allowing Afonso Henriques and his crusaders to enter the castle, has a durable grip on the Lisboetan imagination. The gate where his unverified deed took place bears his name, as does a central Lisbon square below the castle.

Before it was restored, the Castle was a jumble of army and government buildings.

🔟 Mosteiro dos Jerónimos

Few of Lisbon's monuments are overly grand – and while this historic monastery is imposing, its proportions remain approachable. Built from the beginning of the 16th century by Diogo de Boytac and finally by Jerónimo de Ruão, Jerónimos is a celebration of Portugal's territorial expansion and an expression of a uniquely national style. It's also a monument to Portuguese identity, housing tombs of men who helped make the country great, including navigator Vasco da Gama, Dom Sebastião and Luís de Camões.

Manuleine cloister

🕐 This is one of the most visited sites in Lisbon. Think twice before going at weekends, on mid-mornings or on mid-afternoons (the latter two are favoured by tour groups). Hit it at lunchtime, or just before it closes, when the stone turns honey-coloured.

🍷 One of the most serene places for a drink in Belém is the terrace café at the CCB *(see p34)*, overlooking the river from a minimalist garden.

- Praça do Império
- Map B6
- 21 362 00 34
- Open 10am–6pm (4:30pm Oct–Apr) Tue–Sun; closed 25 Dec, 1 Jan, 1 May, Easter Sun
- Adm €6 (concessions €3; under-14s free; free before 2pm on Sun & public holidays)
- www.mosteiro jeronimos.pt

Top 10 Features
1. South Portal
2. West Portal
3. Nave
4. Cloister
5. Refectory
6. Tombs of Vasco da Gama and Luís de Camões
7. Tombs of Dom Sebastião and Cardinal D. Henrique
8. Chancel
9. Chapterhouse
10. Extension

South Portal
Restraint might not be the word for this towering sculpture of an entrance *(above)*, but look closely and you'll see that none of its parts is overpoweringly large. The figures include Henry the Navigator.

West Portal
The mouldings and surrounds of this portal (used today as the main entrance) by French sculptor Nicolau Chanterène show the Manueline love of fantastical Renaissance decoration.

Nave
Many visitors find the well-lit nave *(above)* the most striking feature of Jerónimos, with its soaring pillars supporting a beautiful fan-vaulted ceiling.

Cloister
Begun by Diogo de Boytac and finished by João de Castilho and Diogo de Torralva, the cloister is a lesson in Manueline tracery and lavish ornament *(left)*.

The tomb of Dom Sebastião is empty, as the young king's body was never found after the battle of Alcácer-Quivir.

Refectory

The long, narrow refectory features fabulous vaulting and rope-like Manueline mouldings. The panel on the north wall depicts the biblical story of the feeding of the 5,000.

Entrance

Tombs of Vasco da Gama and Luís de Camões

In the Lower Choir – facing the aisles under the gallery – are the tombs of Vasco da Gama (left) and Luís de Camões (right), transferred here in 1940.

Tombs of Dom Sebastião and Cardinal D. Henrique

As you pass under the stellar vault of the crossing, look to each side to see the grand tombs of Cardinal D. Henrique and Dom Sebastião (above).

Chancel

The current Chancel, dating from 1572, has a gridlike Mannerist layout. Look here for the tombs of Dom Manuel I and his wife Dona Maria (on the left) and Dom III and his wife Dona Catarina (on the right).

Chapterhouse

Completed only in the 19th century, the attractive chapterhouse was never used as such. It houses the tomb of Alexandre Herculano, a celebrated 19th-century historian who also served as the first mayor of Belém.

Stone surprises

Spend some time studying the carvings on the pillars in the nave, and you may come across exotic plants and animals along with exquisite human faces and a few mythical figures. What better way to remind posterity that all this beauty was hewn by human hands, belonging to individuals and masons who would occasionally get bored, when carving.

Extension

Major restoration and extension works in the 19th century saw the addition of the long, Neo-Manueline west wing (below), which now houses the Museu de Arqueologia and part of the Museu da Marinha (see p84). Another addition was the distinctive domed belltower (the previous roof was pointed).

For more examples of the Manueline style See p33

Sé Catedral

Lisbon's cathedral was built shortly after Dom Afonso Henriques had taken Lisbon from the Moors in 1147, and stands on on the site once occupied by the city's main mosque. The crenellated Romanesque building we see today is a restoration and reconstruction, because the cathedral suffered damage from earthquakes and was rebuilt in various architectural fashions. The Sé is also an important archeological site, with new finds made regularly beneath the cloister – originally excavated to reinforce the building's foundations.

Rose window

🕐 The Sé is a very dark church, and enlightenment seems a distant prospect. Much of interest in the chapels is literally obscured. Head for the lighter cloister, and go in the afternoon, when the low light enters the façade's rose window.

🍷 A great place for a relaxed drink in the neighbourhood is Pois, Café *(see p60)*, whose Austrian owners are helping to keep Alfama cosmopolitan.

• Largo da Sé
• Map G4
• 21 886 67 52
• Cloister: open 9am–7pm Mon–Sat, 2–5pm Sun. Adm €2.50 (concessions €1.25)
• Treasury: open 10am–5pm Mon–Sat. Adm €2.50 (concessions €1.25)

Top 10 Features

1. Rose Window
2. Belltowers
3. Romanesque Nave
4. Gothic Ambulatory Chapels
5. Capela de Bartolomeu Joanes
6. St Anthony's Font
7. Cloister
8. 13th-century Iron Railing
9. Archeological Finds
10. Treasury

Rose Window
Reconstructed using parts of the original, the rose window *(above left)* softens the façade's rather severe aspect, but unfortunately lets in only a limited amount of light.

Belltowers
These stocky towers – defining features of the Sé – echo those of Coimbra's cathedral, built a few years earlier by the same master builder, Frei Roberto. A taller third tower over the crossing collapsed in the 1755 earthquake *(see p32)*.

Romanesque Nave
Little remains of the original cathedral beyond the renovated nave. It gives onto a chancel enclosed by an ambulatory, a 14th-century addition.

Gothic Ambulatory Chapels
The Chapel of São Cosme and São Damião is one of nine on the ambulatory. Look out for the tombs of nobleman Lopo Fernandes Pacheco *(above)* and his wife, Maria Villalobos.

Entrance

5 Capela de Bartolomeu Joanes
This Gothic chapel, sponsored by a wealthy Lisbon merchant in 1324, contains the founder's tomb and the 15th-century Renaissance retable *(above)*, painted by Cristóvão de Figueiredo, Garcia Fernandes and Diogo de Contreiras.

6 St Anthony's Font
Tradition has it that Fernando Martins Bulhões (later St Anthony) was baptized in this font – which now bears a tile panel of the saint preaching to the fishes. He is also said to have had his early education at the cathedral school.

7 Cloister
The Gothic cloister, reached through one of the ambulatory's chapels, was an early addition to the Sé. Some of its decoration anticipates the Manueline style.

8 13th-century Iron Railing
One of the ambulatory chapels is closed off by a 13th-century iron railing *(left)*, the only one of its kind to survive in Portugal.

9 Archeological Finds
Remains left by Moors, Visigoths, Romans and Phoenicians have been found in the excavation of the cloister *(right)*.

10 Treasury
The first-floor Treasury is a museum of religious art, with some important holdings. Its most famous treasure, the relics of St Vincent *(see p32)*, was lost in the 1755 earthquake.

Fascinating finds from Lisbon's past
Archeologically, the Sé is a work in progress – as are the castle *(see pp8–9)* and many other parts of central Lisbon. What is most exciting about all this digging is that ever more ancient and striking remains are being uncovered. Public information can lag behind archeological breakthroughs – make a point of asking, and you may be treated to a glimpse of the latest find from Lisbon's past.

For more Lisbon places of worship See pp32–3

Museu Nacional de Arte Antiga

Lisbon's Museu Nacional de Arte Antiga is Portugal's national gallery, a treasure trove of historically illuminating art. Once associated with a certain fustiness, it has recently been sweeping out the cobwebs. Head broom-bearer has been the new director, Dalila Rodrigues, who, in the quest for new types of visitor, has introduced previously unheard-of events such as fashion shows, parties and late-night openings. Private sponsors are another innovation. Critics have been silenced by a rise in visitor numbers of nearly one-third.

Adoration of St Vincent, detail

🔎 There is a lot to look at here. As with any large museum with a wide-ranging collection, study the layout and decide what to concentrate on. For 15 minutes with Nuno Gonçalves or Hieronymus Bosch, it may well be worth giving the world's largest collection of 18th-century French silverware a miss; or vice versa.

🍴 For lunch or dinner, an alternative to the museum cafeteria is Nariz de Vinho Tinto, a short but steep climb up Rua do Conde opposite the museum *(see p89)*.

- Rua das Janelas Verdes
- Map E5
- 21 391 28 00
- 10am–6pm Wed–Sun, 2–6pm Tue
- Admission €4 (concessions €2; under-14s free; free before 2pm Sun & public holidays)
- www.mnarteantiga-ipmuseus.pt

Top 10 Features

1. The Adoration of St Vincent
2. The Temptations of St Anthony
3. St Jerome
4. St Augustine
5. Conversation
6. Capela das Albertas
7. Japanese Screens
8. Portuguese and Chinese Ceramics
9. Indo-Portuguese Furniture
10. Garden/Cafeterias/Shop

1 The Adoration of St Vincent
Arguably the most important Portuguese painting, this polyptych of around 1470 (probably by Nuno Gonçalves) portrays rich and poor in historically fascinating detail.

3 St Jerome
This unusual portrait *(above)* transcends the conventions of religious art. Painted in 1521 by Albrecht Dürer – who used a 93-year-old Antwerp man as his model – it is above all a portrayal of old age.

2 The Temptations of St Anthony
Hieronymus Bosch's three-panelled feast of fear and fantasy *(above)* is one of the museum's treasures – and one of the world's great paintings.

4 St Augustine
This mid-15th century work by Piero della Francesca was identified in 1946 as the missing panel of an altarpiece painted for the church of St Augustine in Borgo San Sepolcro, Italy. Note the crystal staff.

5 Conversation
Pieter de Hooch was a genre painter whose treatment of light was perhaps more complex than that of his contemporary, Vermeer. This work shows his key qualities as an artist.

➜ *One of the figures depicted in the Adoration of St Vincent is said to be the likely artist, Nuno Gonçalves.*

Key
- Second floor
- First floor
- Ground floor

Capela das Albertas
Find your way to the annexe to see the restored chapel of the former Carmelite convent of Santo Alberto, decorated with blue and white *azulejos*.

Japanese Screens
After encountering Portuguese travellers in the 16th century, Japan's artists portrayed them as *namban-jin*, or "southern barbarians". The screens were not meant to be shown outside Japan.

Portuguese and Chinese Ceramics
The museum's 7,500-piece collection of ceramics illustrates the interplay of influences. From the 16th century, Portuguese faïence shows traces of Ming, while Chinese porcelain features coats of arms and other Portuguese motifs.

Indo-Portuguese Furniture
The most interesting of the museum's furniture collections is probably the group of Indo-Portuguese pieces. The *contadores* are many-drawered chests that combine orderliness on top with decorative abandon below.

Garden/ Cafeterias/ Shop
The museum's downstairs cafeteria gives onto a pleasant garden overlooking the river; upstairs is another café and a well-stocked gift shop.

La Nuit des Musées
If you are visiting Lisbon in May, take the opportunity to visit this museum at night, to enjoy a programme of concerts and other events – not least the guided midnight tours. Part of a Europe-wide French initiative to make museum visits something more than quiet Sunday afternoon outings, La Nuit des Musées gives access to the museum's treasures in a new and quite different context.

箇 Parque das Nações

Built on the site of Lisbon's successful Expo 98 world exposition, held to mark the 500th anniversary of Vasco da Gama's epic voyage to India, the "Park of the Nations" is a new, self-contained riverside district east of the centre. It has Belém to it's west and showcases Portuguese architecture of a younger era. A bustling amusement park and trade-fair centre by day, by night the park becomes a concert and events venue, with a young nightlife scene and a recently opened casino. There's also an ambitious residential development.

Boardwalk

🕑 Early mornings in the Parque can be very refreshing, while summer afternoons are hotter, brighter and more humid here than in most other parts of the city. The undulating lawn area next to the Oceanário is a good spot for a rest, as are the benches along the riverfront.

🍹 Drinks can be bought at kiosks dotted around the Parque.

- Avenida Dom João II
- Map C2
- 21 891 98 98
- Oceanário: 21 891 70 02. Open 10am–7pm (6pm in winter) daily. Adm €11 (over-65s €4.75; children 4–12 €5.50; under-4s free). www.oceanario.pt
- Knowledge Pavilion – Ciência Viva: 218 917 112. Open 10am–6pm Tue–Fri, 11am–7pm Sat & Sun. Adm €7 (under-18s and over-65s €4; children 3–6 €3; under-2s free). www.pavconhecimento.pt

Top 10 Features

1. Oceanarium
2. Portugal Pavilion
3. Knowledge Pavilion – Ciência Viva
4. Casino
5. Cable Car
6. Nautical Centre
7. Torre Vasco da Gama
8. Gardens
9. Restaurants
10. Shops

Oceanário
The world's second-largest aquarium *(above)* has hundreds of aquatic species organized by habitat and viewed on two levels. The vast central tank has species large and small, swimming round and round in uneasy peace. Impossibly cuddly-looking sea otters, in a side tank, get the most affection.

Portugal Pavilion
Impressive, with its concrete canopy suspended like a sail above its forecourt, the Portugal Pavilion was once going to house the Council of Ministers. It is now rented out for private functions and special events.

Knowledge Pavilion – Ciência Viva
This large, child-friendly science museum, is full of interactive exhibits *(left)*, experiments and activities for various age groups.

Casino
The latest addition to the Parque das Nações, in the former Future Pavilion, caters to all categories of gambler, with serried ranks of tinkling slot machines and green baize tables for poker, roulette and black jack.

Cable Car

5 Running most of the length of the Parque above the riverside, the cable car ride *(below)* gives an overview of the area and good views of the river and the Vasco da Gama bridge. If the breeze is up on the estuary, the cars may swing from side to side.

Nautical Centre

6 The Doca dos Olivais nautical centre rents out equipment for various water sports *(above)* and related activities.

Torre Vasco da Gama

7 At 145 m (476 ft), this is Lisbon's tallest building *(left)*, albeit removed from the rest of the urban sky-line. On a good day, views from the top extend as far as Setúbal. It is due to open as a hotel in 2010.

Gardens

8 Many of the rather anaemic-looking gardens planted for Expo 98 have grown into healthy patches of urban greenery. They now succeed in softening the concrete and steel, particularly along the waterfront *(below)*.

Restaurants

9 The wide range of over 40 waterfront restaurants are popular for weekend lunches *(below)*, but they are also an important part of the Parque's nightlife scene.

Shops

10 Most shops are in the Vasco da Gama shopping centre, but retailing is developing elsewhere in the Parque. Electronics and interior decoration showrooms are now in operation, and when the FIL trade-fair area – formerly the Expo's national pavilions – puts on a consumer fair, plenty of customers turn up to see the latest offers.

Card Advantages

The Cartão do Parque costs €17.50 for adults and €9 for children and pensioners. It includes one free visit to the Oceanarium and Ciência Viva, one round-trip in a cable car, a ride on the mini-train, and discounts for bicycle hire. The Cartão do Parque is valid for one month. However, it can only be bought at the main visitors' kiosk located at the entrance.

Torre de Belém

The defensive tower at Belém is a jewel of the Manueline architectural style, combining Moorish, Renaissance and Gothic elements in a dazzling whole. It was built in 1515–20 by Francisco de Arruda, probably to a design by Diogo Boitac. At the time of its construction, the tower stood on an island in the river Tejo, about 200 m (650 ft) from the northern riverbank, and so commanded the approach to Lisbon more fully than it does today. The land between the tower and the Jerónimos monastery has since been reclaimed from the river.

Portuguese coat of arms

🕐 The tower is at its prettiest in the early morning or late afternoon. Tour groups tend to go early, so go as late as you can for a quieter visit.

🍴 Nearby restaurants (including Vela Latina – *see p85*) often fill up quickly; if you can't find a table here, cross the railway line by the footbridge and walk to the nearby Centro Cultural de Belém *(see p84)* and the pleasant Jardim das Oliveiras outdoor café.

- Avda Brasilia
- Map A6
- 21 362 00 34
- Open 10am–5pm (6pm May–Sep) Tue–Sun
- Admission €4 (concessions €1.50; senior citizens €3; under-14s free)
- www.mosteiro jeronimos.pt/index_torre. html

Top 10 Features

1. Battlements
2. Renaissance Loggia
3. Governor's Room
4. Dungeon
5. Watchtowers
6. Virgin and Child Sculpture
7. Rhinoceros Detail
8. Manueline Details
9. Armillary Spheres
10. Exhibitions

Battlements
The merlons of most of the tower's battlements are decorated with the cross of the Order of Christ, carved to look like features on a shield. The smaller merlons at the rear and on top of the tower are crowned with pyramid-shaped spikes.

Renaissance Loggia
An arcaded loggia overlooks the main deck – comparisons to a ship are unavoidable here. The loggia breaks with the military style of most of the building and adds a theatrical element, while the railing and tracery of the balustrade *(right)* are pure Manueline. Balconies on each side of the tower echo the loggia's style.

Governor's Room
Now empty, this room *(left)* is where the tower's first governor, Gaspar de Paiva, discharged his duties. After it became obsolete, lighthouse keepers and customs officials worked here. The room's acoustics amplify the slightest whisper.

Lovers of the nautical and military should visit Museu da Marinha in Belém (see p84) and Museu Militar by Santa Apolónia station.

4 Dungeon
From the tower's vaulted bottom level – also used as a dungeon – 16 cannon covered the approaches to Lisbon.

5 Watchtowers
You can't miss the Moorish-influenced watchtowers *(below)*. Their domes are seated on Manueline rope-like circles and rise to a pile of small spheres reminiscent of the tops of chess pieces.

7 Rhinoceros Detail
Each of the sentry boxes is supported by a naturalistically carved stone. The rhinoceros at the base of the north-western box is the most famous, as it is thought to be the first European representation of that animal – but time and the weather have made it look like a pig.

6 Virgin and Child Sculpture
A statue of Our Lady of Safe Homecoming stands by the light well that was used to lower cannon into the dungeon. She evokes not only the intrepid explorers of Portugal's past, but also everyday sailors – and a concern for absent husbands and sons that is one of the roots of the longing of *saudade*.

Holy Namesake
Belém means Bethlehem – and the name is taken from a chapel dedicated to St Mary of Bethlehem, built in the mid-15th century near the river's edge in what was then Restelo. This chapel subsequently gave way to the grand Jerónimos church and monastery; the church is still known as Santa Maria de Belém. The name Restelo, for its part, now applies to the area above and behind Belém, a leafy district of fine residences and embassy buildings.

8 Manueline Details
Ropes and knots were the main theme for the Manueline masons here. The tracery of some of the balustrades features the near-organic shapes *(right)* that would be developed in later Manueline buildings.

9 Armillary Spheres
The armillary spheres carved above the loggia were instruments for showing the motion of the stars around the earth. They became a symbol of Portugal, and still feature on the national flag.

10 Exhibitions
The tower's former dungeon, now quite bright, is often used for temporary exhibitions, as well as for a permanent information display for visitors and a gift shop.

The Manueline style is named after Dom Manuel I (known as The Fortunate), who was king at the height of the era of discovery.

🔟 Museu Nacional do Azulejo

Ceramic tiles, or azulejos, are a distinctive aspect of Portuguese culture, featuring in contexts both mundane and sacred. The art of making them is a Moorish inheritance, much adapted – most noticeably in the addition of human figurative motifs, which Islam forbids. This museum dedicated to tiles is enjoyable both for the excellent displays and for its beautiful setting, a 16th-century convent transformed over the centuries to include some of the city's prettiest cloisters and one of its most richly decorated churches.

Portuguese "carpet" tiles

🕐 The rather awkward location of the Tile Museum can be turned into an asset if you combine it with a visit to Parque das Nações (see p16–17), a shopping trip to Santa Apolónia (see p41), or lunch at D'Avis (see p61).

🍷 The best place for a pleasant drink in this neighbourhood is the museum's own cafeteria; otherwise, head for Santa Apolónia (see p41).

• Rua da Madre de Deus 4
• Map C2
• 21 810 03 40
• Open 2–6pm Tue; 10am–6pm Wed–Sun
• Admission €4
• www.mnazulejo-ipmuseus.pt

Top 10 Features

1. Lisbon Panel
2. Moorish Tiles
3. Manueline Cloister
4. Madre de Deus Church
5. Nossa Senhora da Vida Altarpiece
6. Renaissance Cloister
7. Tile-making Exhibit
8. Temporary Exhibitions
9. Shop
10. Cafeteria and Winter Garden

2 Moorish Tiles

With their attractive geometrical patterns, varied colour palettes, and glazing techniques, Moorish tiles continue to be an inspiration to tile-makers and home decorators alike.

3 Manueline Cloister

This small but stunning cloister *(above)* is one of the few surviving features of the original convent of Madre de Deus. This is the Manueline style at its most restrained. The geometrical wall tiles were added in the 17th century.

1 Lisbon Panel

On the second floor of the main cloister and 23 m (75 ft) long, this vast tiled panorama of Lisbon *(below)* is a captivating depiction of the city's waterfront as it looked in about 1740, before the great earthquake. It was transferred here from one of the city's palaces.

4 Madre de Deus Church

The magnificent barrel-vaulted convent church is the result of three centuries of construction and decoration *(left)*, and contains enough paintings to fill a gallery. Today's layout dates from the 16th century. The tile panels are from the 17th and 18th, as is the Baroque gilt woodwork and other expressions of wealth.

6 Renaissance Cloister

Part of the first major alterations to the convent in the 16th century, this airy, simple cloister on two levels *(below)* is the work of Diogo de Torralva. Now glassed in to protect collections and visitors alike from extremes of weather, it remains the light heart of the building.

5 Nossa Senhora da Vida Altarpiece

Almost 5 m (16 ft) square and containing over 1,000 tiles, this 16th-century Mannerist altarpiece by Marçal de Matos *(above)* shows the Adoration of the Shepherds, flanked by St Luke and St John.

Key

	Second floor
	First floor
	Ground floor

7 Tile-making Exhibit

Step-by-step exhibits of tile-making, from a lump of clay to the final glazing, help visitors to see how the medium combines practical uses with decorative ends.

8 Temporary Exhibitions

The ground and first floors are devoted to temporary exhibitions – like contemporary tile art, an important category in Portugal.

9 Shop

A large selection of quality reproductions of classic tile designs are available, as well as modern tiles and other gift items.

10 Cafeteria and Winter Garden

Suitably tiled with food-related motifs *(left)*, the museum cafeteria is worth a light lunch stop or a coffee. The courtyard is partly covered and acts as a winter garden.

A Nod from the 19th Century

When the southern façade of the church was restored in the late 19th century, the architect used as his model a painting, part of the Retábulo de Santa Auta, now in the Museu de Arte Antiga *(see pp14–15)*. This shows the convent and church as they looked in the early 16th century. Indoors, the quest for authenticity was less zealous. In one of the cloisters, 19th-century restorers have left a potent symbol of their own era: an image of a steam locomotive, incorporated into one of the upper-level capitals.

Lisbon's Top 10

⑩ Palácio de Queluz

Queluz is like a miniature Versailles – an exquisite Rococo palace with formal gardens and parkland, just 15 minutes from central Lisbon. Prince Pedro, younger son of Dom João V, had it built as a summer palace in 1747–52. Thirteen years later, when he married his niece the future Dona Maria I, he commissioned Jean-Baptiste Robillon to design extensions to make it the permanent royal residence. Queluz had a brief golden era before the royal family fled to Brazil after Napoleon's invasion in 1807.

Statue of sphinx in garden

🔂 An early-morning visit to Queluz can be usefully combined with a trip to Sintra *(see pp26–7)*, but remember that Sintra's national palace is closed on Wednesdays, unlike other monuments and museums.

🍷 The terrace at the Pousada is easily the best place for a drink – unless you have an invitation to an event in the palace itself.

• Largo do Palácio
• Map A1
• 21 434 38 60
• Open 9am–5pm Wed–Mon; gardens open later
• Admission €5 (concessions €2.50; under-14s free)

Top 10 Features

1. Gardens
2. Robillon Pavilion
3. Don Quixote Chamber
4. Lion Staircase
5. Sala dos Embaixadores
6. Corredor das Mangas
7. Chapel
8. Music Room
9. Throne Room
10. Cozinha Velha and Pousada Dona Maria I

Gardens
Two formal gardens, the Neptune Garden and Malta Garden, fill the space between the palace's two asymmetric wings. Laid out by a Dutch landscape architect, they once included a small bullring.

Lion Staircase
This beautifully flowing staircase *(above)* links the lower parkland area to the palace and formal gardens. It is flanked by an arcaded "dwarf gallery" with a water cascade flowing into a tiled canal; here, the royal family went boating.

Robillon Pavilion
This warmly pink building *(left)*, replete with windows, balustrades and pillars, is a bit too fussy and overloaded for purists. It was designed by French architect Robillon.

Don Quixote Chamber
The inlaid circular-pattern floor and domed ceiling make this square room *(below)* look round. It is named for painted scenes from *Don Quixote*.

5 Sala dos Embaixadores

The magnificent Ambassadors' Room *(below)* was used for diplomatic audiences, and is opulently decorated with stucco work and painted and gilded carved woodwork. The *trompe l'oeil* ceiling depicts the royal family at a concert, for which purpose the room was also used.

Entrance

6 Corredor das Mangas

The hallway linking the old and newer parts of Queluz was named for the glass cylinders, or sleeves (*mangas*), of its candles. It is also called the *Corredor dos Azulejos*, after its painted wall tiles *(below)*.

7 Chapel

The chapel was the first part of the palace to be completed, in 1752. It was also used for concerts, some by Dona Maria I's own chamber orchestra. She and her sisters are said to have painted some of the wall panels.

8 Music Room

The Music Room *(left)* was used for concerts and even opera performances, and doubled as a venue for important christenings. It still acts as a concert venue.

9 Throne Room

Competing in grandeur with the Ambassadors' Room, and with a magnificent oval, domed ceiling, the Throne Room also served as ballroom, church and theatre – and for lying-in-state.

10 Cozinha Velha and Pousada Dona Maria I

The old palace kitchens have long housed the fine Cozinha Velha restaurant *(right)*. The newer Pousada Dona Maria I, in the former quarters of the Royal Guard, is as close as you'll get to living at Queluz.

The Wailing Queen

Dona Maria I, after she became queen and then lost a son, famously lost her mind. Visitors described hearing her wailing as she wandered the corridors of Queluz. She was exiled to Brazil in 1807 with her younger son, then Regent, to escape the invasion led by the French Emperor Napoleon.

For details of Pousada Dona Maria I **See p114**

TOP 10 Museu Calouste Gulbenkian

Based on the private collections of oil millionaire Calouste Gulbenkian, this museum spans over 4,000 years of art history while remaining marvellously manageable for the visitor. Internationally recognized for the quality of its collections and premises, the museum is part of an attractive 1960s complex that houses the headquarters of the Calouste Gulbenkian Foundation and also includes a concert hall and auditoria for its orchestra, choir, other exhibition spaces, a peaceful park and a modern art museum.

Statue of Calouste Gulbenkian

Taking in another museum in one day might be pushing it, but the Centro de Arte Moderna José Azeredo Perdigão – also part of the Gulbenkian Foundation – has a good collection of contemporary Portuguese art, and stages frequent temporary shows.

There are good cafés at both museums.

- Avenida de Berna 45A
- Map F1
- 21 782 30 00
- Open 10am–5:45pm Tue–Sun
- Admission €4; ticket to both museums €7 (children free, 50% discount for students and over-65s; free on Sun) • www.museu.gulbenkian.pt

Top 10 Features

1. 3rd-dynasty Egyptian Bowl
2. 5thC BC Greek Vase
3. Oriental Islamic Art
4. Yüan Dynasty Stem Cup
5. Portrait of an Old Man
6. St Catherine and St Joseph
7. Louis XV and XVI furniture
8. Boy Blowing Bubbles
9. Diana Statue
10. Lalique collection

1 3rd-dynasty Egyptian Bowl

Found in a tomb north of Thebes, this simple, elegant alabaster bowl was modelled on an everyday ointment bowl. The ancient Egyptians adorned tombs with such copies of everyday objects made from noble materials. This one is 4,000 years old.

2 5thC BC Greek Vase

This beautiful, wide-rimmed terracotta vase *(right)* is decorated with mythological motifs: the abduction of Phoebe and Hilaira by Castor and Pollux, and a bacchanalian scene.

3 Oriental Islamic Art

A large gallery shows a wide-ranging collection of manuscripts, carpets *(right)*, textiles, ceramics and other objects from Turkey, Syria, the Caucasus (including Gulbenkian's birthplace Armenia), Persia and India.

4 Yüan Dynasty Stem Cup

This rare blue-glazed piece dates from an earlier period (1279–1368) than most of the Far Eastern collection. It is decorated with delicate high-relief cutouts of Taoist figures under bamboo leaves.

5 Portrait of an Old Man

Entrance

This engaging *chiaroscuro* portrait of a bearded man *(left)* is an example of Rembrandt's preoccupation at that time with ageing. The gaze is tired, and the large hands intricately lined but held in a relaxed manner. Nothing is known about the model.

6 St Catherine and St Joseph

Two paintings by the 15th-century Flemish master Rogier van der Weyden are believed to be parts of an altarpiece; a third element is in London's National Gallery. The female figure *(below)* is thought to be St Catherine of Alexandria.

7 Louis XV and XVI Furniture

Considered ostentatious and over-decorated by some, the 18th-century French pieces *(above)* in the decorative art collection fascinate for their materials and crafts-manship. Stars include a Louis XV chest inlaid with Japanese lacquer panels, gold leaf, mother-of-pearl, bronze and ebony; and a table with folding flaps and a shelf that flips over to reveal a mirror.

8 Boy Blowing Bubbles

Édouard Manet's 1867 painting *(main picture)* is not just a version of the popular allegory on the transience of life and art, but a deftly and freely painted portrait of Léon-Édouard Koëlla, Manet's stepson.

9 Diana Statue

A graceful marble 1780 statue *(right)* by the French sculptor Jean-Antoine Houdon is unusual for the era in that it depicts the goddess in movement, and completely naked. It belonged to Catherine the Great of Russia and was exhibited at the Hermitage, where its nudity caused scandal and notoriety.

10 Lalique Collection

Gulbenkian was a close friend of the French Art Nouveau jeweller René Lalique, and bought many of his graceful pieces. In fact, this part of the museum has almost too many.

The Spoils of Oil

Calouste Sarkis Gulbenkian was an Armenian who made a huge fortune negotiating the transfer of assets between oil companies – each time earning a five per cent commission. He came to Lisbon during World War II, staying at the Hotel Aviz until his death in 1955. His will stipulated that a foundation be set up in Portugal to care for his vast collection and to support the arts.

Sintra

Recognized in 1995 as a UNESCO World Heritage Site, Sintra was the summer retreat of Portuguese kings from the 13th to the late 19th centuries. It still possesses many of the classic qualities of a hill station: a cooler climate than the city, ample greenery and an atmosphere conducive to indulging romantic whims. The older town is pretty but crowded, and the surrounding landscapes and sights are an essential part of any visit. Access from Lisbon is straightforward, by motorway or by train from Rossio Station.

Window, Palácio Nacional

Sintra's romantic and refreshing qualities may be seriously challenged on summer weekends, when tour groups and locals collide in the square in front of the Palácio Nacional. Go during the week, and avoid the middle of the day in summer.

Bars and cafés in the old town fill up quickly and charge inflated prices. For a different atmosphere, walk past the Tourist Office to Lawrence's Hotel and have a drink in one of its small, colonial-cosy public rooms.

• Tourist information: Praça da República 23, Sintra. 21 923 11 57 www.cm-sintra.pt
• Sintra lies 30 km (18 miles) northwest of Lisbon. Trains run frequently from Lisbon's Rossio and Entrecampos Station.

Top 10 Features

1. Palácio Nacional
2. Castelo dos Mouros
3. Palácio da Pena
4. Parque da Pena
5. Quinta da Regaleira
6. Parque da Liberdade
7. Museu do Brinquedo
8. São Pedro Market
9. Palácio de Seteais
10. Monserrate

Castelo dos Mouros
The 8th-century castle *(above)* seems to hover above the town between boulder-littered crags. It was captured from the Moors by Afonso Henriques in 1147. Dom Fernando II partially rebuilt it in the 19th century. Inside are a ruined chapel and a Moorish cistern.

Palácio Nacional
Twin chimneys mark the former royal palace *(below)*. Begun in the 14th century and altered and extended in the 16th, it is a captivating mix of styles from the Moorish to the Baroque.

Palácio da Pena
Dom Fernando II, Dona Maria II's German-born king consort, had this fabulous toyland palace *(left)* built in the mid-19th century. The intriguing work of a hyperactive imagination, it exhibits all his eclectic and romantic tastes, and has been preserved as it was when the royal family last lived there.

4 Parque da Pena
Filled with exotic trees and shrubs, the park around the Palácio da Pena is another of Dom Fernando II's contributions to Sintra's romantic magic. It contains the chalet he had built for his mistress, a German opera singer whom he later married.

5 Quinta da Regaleira
This lavish palace *(left)* looms up on a steep bend in the old road to Sintra. It was built around 1900 for António Augusto Carvalho Monteiro, an eccentric millionaire. He was a bibliophile and keen dabbler in alchemy and other esoteric subjects.

6 Parque da Liberdade
The tree-thronged town park with a variety of tree species and steep steps and paths occupies the top of the valley below the old town.

7 Museu do Brinquedo
One man's extensive toy collection from the 1930s on *(above)* is housed in the old fire station. It has a toy restoration workshop and a small shop.

Artistic Treasures
Sintra's Museu de Arte Moderna, a partnership between Madeiran art collector José Berardo and Sintra municipality, houses the Berardo collection, one of the biggest private collections of modern art in the world. The collection showcases productions from the main movements in modern art and also has some contemporary pieces from artists of the 21st century. Visitors can access the Museum via regular trains departing from Rosso Station in central Lisbon to Sintra.

8 São Pedro Market
Antiques are a feature of the lively market held in the suburb of São Pedro on the second and fourth Sundays of each month.

9 Palácio de Seteais
Built in 1787, Seteais (now a hotel) got its neo-classical façade later. It's best to visit, well dressed, for tea or a meal.

10 Monserrate
The beautiful gardens of Monserrate, with their fantastic Moorish-style palace *(right)* and exotic plants, were laid out by English residents.

English poet Lord Byron, an early visitor to Monserrate, extolled the beauty of the place in his Childe Harold's Pilgrimage.

Left **Lisbon recaptured, 1147** Centre **Monument to the Restoration** Right **Birth of the Republic**

🔟 Moments in History

1 138 BC: Roman Occupation
Although they had reached the Iberian peninsula in the second century BC, the Romans did not conquer its westernmost parts until nearly a century later. The trading post of Olisipo, Lisbon's Greek name (sometimes associated with Ulysses), was occupied in 138 BC.

2 714: Moorish Occupation
Roman Lisbon was invaded by Alan tribes from the north, about whom little is known, and then by the Visigoths, who ruled from Toledo. Less than three centuries after the end of Roman rule, however, the Visigoths were swept from power by Moorish armies crossing into Iberia at the Straits of Gibraltar. Lisbon fell to the Moors in 714.

3 1147: Reconquest
The Christian reconquest of the Iberian peninsula from the Moors began in the north, where Afonso Henriques founded the Portuguese kingdom – as distinct from the future Spanish kingdom of León – in 1140. His armies reached Lisbon in 1147 and took the city following a three-month seige.

Tomb of Vasco da Gama

4 1497: Vasco da Gama Sails from Belém
The crowning achievement of Portugal's era of discovery and expansion was Vasco da Gama's well-documented, nearly year-long voyage to India. Rounding the Cape of Good Hope, he proved Columbus wrong and gave the Portuguese the competitive edge in the spice trade.

5 1640: Independence from Spain
Spain had usurped the Portuguese throne in 1581, after the death of Dom Sebastião and much of the Portuguese nobility in an ill-conceived military adventure in north Africa. The 1640 coup at Lisbon's royal palace reinstated self-rule and proclaimed the Duke of Bragança king of Portugal.

6 1755: The Great Earthquake
On 1 November 1755, All Saints' Day, a massive earthquake struck southern Portugal and laid waste to central Lisbon. Three shocks were followed by fires and tidal waves. The scale of the destruction shocked the world.

7 1910: Portugal Becomes a Republic
In 1908, Dom Carlos and his heir were assassinated by republican activists in Terreiro do Paço. The king's surviving son became Dom Manuel II, but abdicated in October 1910 in the face of a republican revolution. The Republic was formalized on 5 October.

Preceding pages **Padrão dos Descobrimentos (Monument to the Discoveries), western face** *(see p84)*

Rescue of an earthquake survivor

1933: The New State
António de Oliveira Salazar, who had been appointed finance minister in the hope that he could solve the country's financial crisis, was asked to form a government in 1932. The following year his new constitution was passed by parliament, in effect making him an authoritarian dictator.

1974: The Carnation Revolution
Salazar's successor Marcelo Caetano and his government were overthrown in a virtually bloodless coup by a group of army captains on 25 April. Three men were killed by shots coming from the headquarters of the PIDE, the political police, as crowds outside cheered the end of its reign of fear.

1986: European Union Membership
After a few tumultuous years following the 1974 revolution, stable democracy was established in Portugal. Independence had already been restored to most of the colonies and Portugal was now ready to turn to Europe. Membership brought a welcome boost to the economy, in the form of both subsidies and foreign investment.

Top 10 Historical Figures

1 Viriato
The legendary leader of the Lusitanians, a Celtic-Iberian tribe that resisted Roman occupation for two decades.

2 Tariq
As Berber leader of the Moorish force, Tariq conquered most of the Iberian peninsula in 711–16.

3 Afonso Henriques
Having taken control of the countship of Portucale, Afonso was calling himself "Portucalense king" by 1140.

4 Henry the Navigator
Son of Dom João, Prince Henry was the architect of Portugal's early overseas expansion in the 15th century.

5 Duke of Bragança
Hesitant at first, he soon agreed to be king, as Dom João IV, after the 1640 coup.

6 Marquis of Pombal
Chief minister under Dom José I, he reconstructed the city after the earthquake, but was later reviled as a despot.

7 Eça de Queiroz
The 19th-century chronicler of Lisbon was a member of the Cenáculo, a group of writers opposed to the monarchy.

8 António de Oliveira Salazar
Portugal's deceptively low-key dictator was originally a professor of economics.

9 Mário Soares
The first democratically elected post-revolution prime minister won a second term and, in 1986, the presidency.

10 Aníbal Cavaco Silva
Leader of the Social Democrats and prime minister from 1985 to 1995, he was elected president in 2005.

The Museu da Sociedade Geográfica (see p66) is full of booty and memorabilia from Portugal's colonial era.

Left **Cloister, Mosteiro dos Jerónimos** Right **Igreja do Carmo**

🔟 Churches and Monasteries

1 Mosteiro dos Jerónimos
The country's most important monument displays the exuberant, almost oriental ornamentation that is a chief characteristic of the Manueline style *(see pp10–11)*.

2 Sé Catedral
Seen at a distance, Lisbon's cathedral can almost conjure up the mosque that preceded it. Up close, the Romanesque building is attractively simple *(see pp12–13)*.

3 Igreja de Santa Engrácia
One of Lisbon's most uplifting churches is an unmistakable feature of the city's eastern skyline. This Baroque beauty is most famous for having taken 284 years to build, but it also houses the cenotaphs to national heroes, hence the groups of schoolchildren clustered around.

Tomb of Maria I, Basílica da Estrela

🚫 *Campo de Santa Clara • Map R3 • 10am–5pm Tue–Sun • Adm charge*

4 Igreja de São Domingos
One of Lisbon's oldest churches is one of its hardiest survivors. Built in 1242, it was damaged by earthquakes in 1531 and 1755, and ravaged by fire in 1959. The blackened interior helps you imagine the days when Inquisition processions would begin here, to end with charred corpses. 🚫 *Largo de São Domingos • Map M3 • 8am–7pm daily • Free*

5 Igreja do Carmo
The late 14th-century church and convent of Carmo was one of Lisbon's main places of worship before the roof caved in on All Saints' Day 1755, killing the congregation. The evocative ruin, with its bare Gothic arches, now houses an archaeological museum. 🚫 *Largo do Carmo • Map L4 • 10am–7pm Mon–Sat (Oct–Apr: 10am–6pm) • Adm charge*

6 Basílica da Estrela
This domed Lisbon landmark was built from 1779 to give thanks for the birth of a son and male heir to Dona Maria I. Sadly, the boy died of smallpox before the church was finished. Inside is the queen's tomb, and a nativity scene with over 500 cork-and-terracotta figures; ask the sacristan to show you it. 🚫 *Praça da Estrela • Map E4 • 8am–8pm daily • Free*

7 Igreja de São Vicente
In 1173, when St Vincent was proclaimed patron saint of Portugal, his relics were moved to the original church on this site. Philip II of Spain had the present Mannerist church built in the early 17th century. As if to prove a point about independence, in 1885 the refectory was turned into the pantheon of the Bragança royal family. 🚫 *Largo de São Vicente • Map Q3 • 9am–5pm Tue–Sat; 9am–1pm Sun • Free*

Among Lisbon's working monasteries is Convento dos Cardeais in Rua do Século.

Igreja de Santo António

Lisbon's patron saint was allegedly born here (as Fernando Bulhões) in the late 12th century. The present Baroque church replaced the one lost to the 1755 earthquake. In June, weddings are held here, as St Anthony is said to bring luck to newly-weds. ◈ *Largo de Santo António à Sé • Map N4 • 8am–7pm daily • Free*

Chapel of St John the Baptist, São Roque

Igreja de São Roque

Built in the 16th century for the Jesuit order, this church is famous for its opulent interior, particularly the Chapel of St John the Baptist. Made in Rome using lapis lazuli, agate, alabaster, amethyst, precious marbles, gold and silver, it was blessed by the pope, taken apart and sent to Lisbon in three ships. ◈ *Largo Trindade Coelho • Map K3 • 8:30am–5pm Mon–Fri; 9:30am–5pm Sat & Sun • Free*

Igreja da Graça

The Augustinian monastery of Graça dates from 1271, but was rebuilt after the 1755 earthquake. The church is home to the *Senhor dos Passos*, a figure of Christ carrying the cross, which is carried in a traditional procession during Lent. ◈ *Largo da Graça • Map P2 • 9:30am–7:30pm (8pm Sun) daily • Free*

Top 10 Manueline Gems

1. **Torre de Belém**
While more decorative than defensive today, this tower is a perfect Manueline gem.

2. **Jerónimos Cloister**
João de Castilho's cloister features the whole Manueline arsenal. Take your time in it.

3. **South Portal of Jerónimos**
This riot of decoration – saints, royals and symbols – is actually completely symmetrical.

4. **Nave of Jerónimos**
Mixing organic elements with geometry, octagonal piers encrusted with carvings rise to the web-like vaulting.

5. **Conceição Velha Portal**
The Manueline portal is the only remnant of the original 16th-century church, destroyed in the 1755 earthquake.

6. **Portal, Museu do Azulejo**
The Manueline portal dates from the 19th century, when the façade was reconstructed from a 16th-century painting.

7. **Manueline Cloister, Museu do Azulejo**
This small, attractive and relatively restrained cloister is a reminder of the building's 16th-century role as a convent.

8. **Ermida de São Jerónimo**
This simple chapel from 1514 gives the Manueline a broader, more contemporary aesthetic.

9. **Casa dos Bicos**
Built as a private palace in 1523, this structure picked up on Italian style as well as including Manueline windows.

10. **Rossio Station**
A nostalgic Neo-Manueline look back from 1892, with a hint of parallels to Art Nouveau.

The early 16th-century Manueline style is an exuberant architectural hybrid of Gothic with Spanish, Flemish and Italian elements.

Left **Lalique glass, Museu Calouste Gulbenkian** Centre **Museu Nacional do Azulejo** Right **CCB**

Museums and Galleries

1 Museu Calouste Gulbenkian
The Armenian oil baron and art collector Calouste Gulbenkian is arguably the single most important person in Portuguese post-war cultural life. His museum is a rare treat because it covers so much in such a manageable way – and also because it has pleasant gardens and a good contemporary arts centre *(see pp24–5)*.

2 Museu Nacional de Arte Antiga
Portugal's national museum provides a home for some priceless national and international icons. As of late it does so in an innovative and unstuffy way. Director Dalila Rodrigues has succeeded in upping visitor numbers by almost a third by unorthodox measures such as throwing parties, staging fashion shows and opening late into the night *(see pp14–15)*.

The Adoration of St Vincent, **Museu Nacional de Arte Antiga**

3 Museu Nacional do Azulejo
Lisbon's tile museum is a tourist favourite, for good reason. It is housed in a stunning convent and church, covers tiles and tile-making comprehensively, and has the bonus of a pleasant café-restaurant *(see pp20–21)*.

4 Museu Nacional dos Coches
A coach museum is the sort of place you might not go to if you didn't have a special interest in the subject. In this case, that would be a mistake. This is one of Lisbon's most highly regarded and popular museums, for its collection of 45 horse-drawn coaches and the connections they create with the past. Praça Afonso de Albuquerque • Map B6 • 21 361 08 50 • 10am–5:30pm Tue–Sun • Adm charge • www.museu doscoches-ipmuseus.pt

5 Centro Cultural de Belém (CCB)
Controversial when it opened in 1992, this starkly modern fortress of culture is now well liked for the breadth of its programme and the relevance of its exhibitions. The CCB hosts a selection of the latest talent in dance, opera, theatre, music and film. Praça do Império • Map A6 • 21 361 24 00 • 10am–7pm Mon–Sun • Adm charge • www.ccb.pt

6 Galeria 111
With over 40 years in the business to its credit, this uptown gallery shows such artists as Paula Rego, Júlio Pomar and Joana Vasconcelos. Campo Grande 113A • off map • 21 797 74 18 • 10am–7pm Mon–Sat • Free

Zé dos Bois

ZDB, as it is also known, has consistently been Lisbon's most inspirational and genuinely "alternative" gallery. It is also a Bairro Alto bar. ® *Rua da Barroca 59* • *Map K4* • *21 343 02 05* • *5–11pm Wed–Sat* • *Free* • *www.zedosbois.org*

Museu do Chiado

Guardian of Portuguese modernity in art, this museum has a collection beginning with Romanticism in the mid-19th century and extending throughout the 20th century, though the latter half is less fully covered. There are also temporary exhibitions and a pleasant courtyard café-restaurant *(see p71)*.

Culturgest

The arts-patronage arm of a bank is one of Lisbon's most active cultural centres, focusing on modern music, dance, cinema, theatre and art. ® *Caixa Geral de Depósitos, Rua Arco do Cego* • *Map G1* • *21 790 51 55* • *Galleries: 11am–7pm Mon & Wed–Fri; 2–8pm Sat & Sun* • *Adm charge* • *www.culturgest.pt*

Fundação/Museu Arpad Szenes-Vieira da Silva

This museum is devoted to the work of Portuguese Modernist Maria Helena Vieira da Silva and her Hungarian husband, Arpad Szenes. ® *Praça das Amoreiras 56–8* • *Map F3* • *21 388 00 44* • *11am–7pm Mon & Wed–Sat; 10am–6pm Sun* • *Adm charge (free on Sun)* • *www.fasvs.pt*

Ornate coach, Museu Nacional dos Coches

Top 10 Portuguese Artists

1 Nuno Gonçalves
He is believed to be the 15th-century painter of *The Adoration of St Vincent*, which may contain his self-portrait.

2 Grão Vasco (Vasco Fernandes)
One of Portugal's best-known 16th-century painters (c.1475–1542) is known for his Flemish-style altarpieces.

3 Josefa de Óbidos
This painter and engraver (1630–84) falls between the Mannerist and the Baroque.

4 Joaquim Machado de Castro
This celebrated sculptor (1731–1822) is best known for his equestrian statue of Dom José I in Praça do Comércio.

5 José Malhoa
A naturalistic painter (1855–1933), creator of the deliciously languorous *O Fado*.

6 Columbano Bordalo Pinheiro
A gifted portraitist, Columbano (1857–1929) painted many of the leading figures of the Republican movement.

7 Júlio Pomar
One of the country's essential 20th-century painters, Pomar (b.1926) was at odds with the Fascist dictatorship.

8 Paula Rego
Rego (b.1935) paints the Portuguese with rare acuity and beauty.

9 João Cutileiro
Portugal's best-known living sculptor (b.1937) has a knack for making marble playful.

10 Joana Vasconcelos
A master of transformation, Vasconcelos (b.1971) creates beauty from mundane items.

Agenda Cultural *(see p107)* is the best guide to current exhibitions.

Left **Café at the top of the Elevador de Santa Justa** Centre **Cristo Rei** Right **Igreja da Graça**

🔟 City Views

Castelo
1 The view from under the umbrella pines on the Castle's esplanade takes in Alfama, the Baixa, Bairro Alto on the hill opposite, and the river. The light here is particularly warm in the late afternoon, encouraging you to linger. ⬡ *Map N3*

Santa Luzia
2 Most tourists head for the nearby Largo das Portas do Sol viewpoint, on the other side of the Santa Luzia church. But this one has all the proper trappings, including a pergola with tiled pillars, walls and benches forming a veranda for the view. There is a café below, but it doesn't have the view. ⬡ *Map P4*

Santa Luzia

São Pedro de Alcântara
3 This small garden is one of Lisbon's best known viewpoints. Bougainvillea tumbles onto the next terrace, a more formal and less accessible garden. The view extends across Restauradores and the Baixa to the Sé and the Castle. ⬡ *Map K2*

Miradouro de Santa Catarina
4 Not just a visual vantage point, this is also a place to meet and hang out. Adamastor, the mythical creature from Camões' epic poem *The Lusiads*, presides over events from a stone plinth. There's a wide view of the river, the station at Cais do Sodré, the Alcântara docks and the 25 de Abril bridge. ⬡ *Map J5*

Igreja da Graça
5 The pine-shaded esplanade by the Graça church has a café with a classic view of the lower city, the river and the bridge. Like the Castle's viewpoint, this one is best visited in the late afternoon. ⬡ *Map P2*

Senhora do Monte
6 One of the highest vantage points in the city, Our Lady of the Mount (there is a small chapel behind the viewpoint) affords a grand vista that includes the Castle, the Graça church and the Mouraria quarter, as well as the Tejo estuary, the lower city, midtown Lisbon and the Monsanto park. ⬡ *Map N1*

➡ *Wander around neighbourhoods such as Lapa and Alfama, and you'll soon find your own viewpoints.*

The view from Castelo

Elevador de Santa Justa

The best close-up overview of the Baixa and Rossio, with the Castle above, is to be had from the terrace at the top of the Elevador de Santa Justa. There is also a café here (charging high prices), but it is worth climbing the last spiral staircase just for the view. ✎ Map M4

Cristo Rei

From his tall perch on the south side of the river, Christ the King spreads his arms to protect Lisbon. The 28-m (92-ft) statue on an 82-m (270-ft) pedestal was inaugurated in 1959 in thanks for Portugal's escape from involvement in World War II. Dubbed "the traffic policeman" when the traffic jams on the bridge were at their worst, the monument is a great vantage point for taking in all of Lisbon and the Tejo estuary. Lifts ascend to the platform beneath the statue. ✎ off map

Jardim do Torel

The Jardim do Torel is a less well

known viewpoint in a small garden on a slope overlooking Restauradores and the Avenida da Liberdade – providing not just a fine view but a great place for quiet contemplation too. ✎ Map L1

Parque Eduardo VII

It's difficult to feel any real affection for Eduardo VII park, with its formal plan, its football-killing slope and its lack of shade, but climb to the top and you will see the architect's idea, as Lisbon stretches away from you in an unbroken perspective right down to the river. The sides offer a less commanding view but more shade and human interest. ✎ Map F2

Cristo Rei was inspired by Rio de Janeiro's emblematic Christ the Saviour statue.

37

Left **Restaurant Moamba** Right **Associação Caboverdeana**

🔟 African Lisbon

1 Associação Caboverdeana
The Cape Verde Association has a restaurant where you can try the one-pot wonders of the islands' cuisine. It's open for lunch only, but there's live music on Tuesdays and Thursdays.
🌐 *Rua Duque de Palmela 2, 8° • Map F3 • 21 353 19 32 • Closed Sat–Sun, D • €*

2 Poço dos Negros Area
This part of Lisbon had connections with the slave trade; later it became a Little Cape Verde, where men from the islands stayed while seeking work. Most of them have now been joined by their families and moved out to the suburbs, but it still has Cape Verdean restaurants, including the legendary Cachupa, and shops. 🌐 *Rua do Poço dos Negros/Rua de São Bento/Rua dos Poiais de São Bento • Map F4*

3 Casa da Morna
Part-owned by Cape Verdean musician Tito Paris, this African restaurant is more upmarket

Poço dos Negros

Restaurant Casa da Morna

than most. It's warmly-painted, windowless but cool, and there's live music most nights. 🌐 *Rua Rodrigues Faria 21 • Map D5 • 21 364 63 99 • Closed Sun, Mon L • €€€*

4 São Cristovão
Cheap, chatty and cheerful, this simple Cape Verdean restaurant near the castle fills stomachs and warms hearts.
🌐 *Rua de São Cristovão 28–30 • Map P3 • 21 888 55 78 • €*

5 Cantinho do Aziz
Aziz, from Mozambique, set up one of Lisbon's smallest and friendliest African restaurants. Now his widow and sons run his *cantinho* (corner), maintaining the feeling that you're eating in someone's frugal but welcoming home. 🌐 *Rua de São Lourenço 3-5 • Map N3 • 21 887 64 72 • €*

6 Enclave
Lisbon's first African disco and restaurant was opened in 1976 by Bana, a Cape Verdean singer, and still serves *cachupas* and *moambas* to the sound of live, hip-wagging music.

  Share your travel recommendations on traveldk.com

The disco starts at midnight, downstairs. ✆ *Rua do Sol ao Rato 71A* • *Map E3* • *21 386 08 77* • *Restaurant closed Tue; disco open Fri & Sat* • €€

7 Mussulo

An Angolan club with a well-dressed clientele dancing close together to *zouk* or to quicker, newer beats. Gets going late at night. ✆ *Rua Sousa Martins 5D* • *Map F2* • *21 355 68 72* • *Closed Mon & Tue*

8 Luanda

This big club in the nightlife area of Alcântara draws a younger crowd – mainly Angolan – dancing to Afro-techno and other music. As in most African clubs, admission is free for women; for men the charge varies. ✆ *Travess Teixeira Júnior 6* • *Map D5* • *Closed Sun–Tue*

Luanda

9 Cantinho da Paz

Goan dishes like veal *xacuti* rub shoulders with African favourites like prawn *moqueca*. Live music on Friday and Saturday nights. ✆ *Rua da Paz 4* • *Map F4* • *21 390 19 63* • *Closed Sun* • €€

10 Moamba

A basic restaurant serving flavoursome dishes of various African origins. The big draw is the signature dish *moamba de galinha*, a chicken stew. Moamba is a short walk from some of the other African places. ✆ *Rua Fradesso da Silveira 75* • *Map D5* • *21 363 03 10* • *Closed Sun* • €€

Top 10 Ex-colonies

1 Angola (1648–1975)
Rich in resources, Angola was Portugal's biggest African colony until its war of liberation. Decades of civil war followed.

2 Mozambique (1885–1975)
Mozambique had been fighting for independence for 15 years when Portugal ceded it.

3 Guinea-Bissau (1446–1974)
This small west African nation declared independence unilaterally in 1973; it was recognized the following year.

4 Cape Verde (1456–1975)
These islands, off west Africa, were unoccupied when the Portuguese first arrived.

5 São Tomé & Príncipe (1522–1975)
These islands in the Gulf of Guinea became one of the world's smallest and poorest independent nations. Oil finds are now boosting the economy.

6 Goa (1510–1961)
Portuguese until annexed by India, it was one of the few colonies where intermarriage created a mixed community.

7 Timor (1511-1975)
Indonesia annexed Timor in 1975; it became independent East Timor in 2002.

8 Ceylon (1517–1658)
The Portuguese occupied parts of today's Sri Lanka until ousted by the Dutch.

9 Macau (1557-1999)
The oldest European colony in China, Macau was Portuguese-ruled for 442 years.

10 Brazil (1500–1822)
By far Portugal's biggest colony, taking many African slaves, Brazil became seat of the Portuguese court in 1808, then declared independence.

One meeting point for the African community in central Lisbon is outside the São Domingos church (see p32).

Left **Art-Nouveau shop, Chiado** Centre **Campo de Ourique food market** Right **Bairro Alto shoe shop**

🔝 Shopping Districts

Rua Augusta shoppers, Baixa

Baixa
The charm of the Baixa lies with its courteous shopkeepers, who still stand behind wooden counters and do sums on bits of paper. For all that, the pedestrianized Rua Augusta is lined with modern chains. ◈ *Map M4–5*

Chiado
Traditionally the quarter with Lisbon's most elegant shops, the Chiado is now the city's most varied and rewarding shopping district. It mixes quiet streets with lively squares and sheet-music suppliers with street-cred fashion boutiques. ◈ *Map L4*

Guerra Junqueiro/Roma
Head uptown to Avda Guerra Junqueiro and adjacent Avda Roma for good clothes shops and cafés – and a visit to *tia* territory. *Tia* means "aunt", but also signifies a deeply tanned, jewellery-laden woman who takes her shopping seriously. ◈ *Map G1*

Campo de Ourique/ Amoreiras
Gentrification proceeds at a genteel pace in Campo de Ourique. The grid street plan makes for lots of corner bakeries, cafés and small shops. The nearby Amoreiras Towers was Lisbon's first shopping centre. Brash and in a more trafficky location, they nevertheless provide plenty to tempt the shopper. ◈ *Map E3*

Fresh Food Markets
Prices at Lisbon's food markets may not be lower than at supermarkets, but the produce is often fresher and the experience has an added flavour. Among the best are Mercado da Ribeira, opposite Cais do Sodré station; Mercado de Campo de Ourique, in west Lisbon; and Mercado 31 de Janeiro, behind the Saldanha Residence building on Avenida Fontes Pereira de Melo. ◈ *Map K6, E3, F2*

Bairro Alto
Bairro Alto competes with the big shopping centres by also offering night-time shopping – in a much cooler setting, and with the possibility of sipping on a drink as you shop. Some shops here may seem ineffably trendy, but Bairro Alto is a proven nursery for Portuguese fashion and design. ◈ *Map K3–4*

Markets open early and pack up at around lunchtime.

7 Rua de São Bento/ Rua da Escola Politécnica

Rua de São Bento is a mini-district for antiques and second-hand shops, among others. It's a short hop to pleasant Praça das Flores, for a coffee under the trees, and then an uphill walk to Rua da Escola Politécnica, where some more expensive antiques shops are clustered. ◈ Map F4

8 Santa Apolónia

Although just a row of converted warehouses, this small shopping area opposite Santa Apolónia station has some of Lisbon's most interesting shops – for music, food and design. They are spiritually presided over by the Bica do Sapato restaurant (see p44) and the adjacent Lux nightclub (see p42). ◈ Map R3

9 Feira da Ladra

Lisbon's Thieves' Market sells items like beautiful brass taps that won't fit any known plumbing. As with most flea markets, it's the sights, sounds, people and haggling that are the thing. ◈ Campo de Santa Clara • Map R2 • Tue, Sat

Feira da Ladra market

10 Avenida da Liberdade

It could be greener and wider, but Lisbon's grand avenue remains torn between its roles as road and promenade. Several international designers are not put off and have their main Lisbon shops here, alongside some venerable local merchants. ◈ Map F3

Top 10 Things to Buy

1 Ceramics
Portuguese ceramics extend beyond tiles to pottery, from the rustic to the twee.

2 Embroidery
Bordados are delicate, but lasting, old-world table linen.

3 Clothes at Markets
Rifle through fakes and failures for the odd find at Cascais on the first or third Sunday of the month, or Carcavelos on any Thursday.

4 Shoes
Fewer shoes are made in Portugal now, but those that are tend to be of higher quality.

5 Stainless Steel Cookware
There are several good-value brands of pots, pans and other kitchen essentials. Look out for Artame and Lourenço.

6 Wine
A wisely spent €5 will get you a truly good wine; €20 an unforgettable one. The wide choice is a pleasant surprise.

7 Cheese
Choose from runny Serra ewes' milk cheeses, delicious Serpa and Azeitão, peppery Castelo Branco and excellent hard and soft goats' cheeses.

8 Hams and Smoked Meats
The best *presunto* (cured ham) was from the north, but the Alentejan ham of the Ibérico pig is arguably better. Taste first, and decide for yourself.

9 Preserved Foods
Sardines and other tinned fish, olives, olive oil, *massa de pimentão* (red-pepper paste) and chilli sauces are all superb.

10 Beauty Treatments
Lisbon's beauty salons are labour-intensive rather than high-tech and offer good value.

One-stop shopping until late at night is available at Lisbon's many shopping malls, including Colombo and Vasco da Gama.

41

Left **Lux** Right **Nova Alcântara**

Bars and Nightclubs

1 Lux
Lux is Lisbon's most stylish and varied nightclub. With a downstairs dance floor, an upstairs bar and dance area, a roof-top terrace, groovy retro decor and a string of hot DJs, there is substance to the hype. ✆ Cais da Pedra, Avenida Infante Dom Henrique • Map R3

2 Nova Alcântara
In the same warehouse premises as the revered 1990s Alcântara-Mar, Nova Alcântara still kicks up a dancing frenzy. ✆ Rua da Cozinha Economica 11 • Map D5

3 Paradise Garage
One of Lisbon's best-known live venues contrasts up-and-coming, occasionally alternative bands with a pretty mainstream club scene on other nights. ✆ Rua João Oliveira Miguéis 38–48 • Map D5

4 Buddha Lx
Not affiliated with other Buddha Bars, but not unlike them either, Buddha Lx offers a cosier, less rigorously designed space in which to soak up its deep-house sounds. The summer terrace is a treat, though the Indian knick-knacks clash with the building's Modernist soul. The first-floor den is reserved for VIPs and big spenders. ✆ Gare Marítima de Alcântara • Map D5

5 Kremlin
Kremlin was the first big dance club in Lisbon and it is still a great place to go if you really want to get down and dance the night away. There is just a whiff of danger about the place; the doormen always seem to be on edge. ✆ Escadinhas da Praia 5 • Map E5

6 Incógnito
This veteran of 18 years has unobtrusively kept on doing what it does best and draws a mostly low-profile crowd. Sized between a bar and a club, it accommodates both chilling and grooving. The music is a mixed bag, with recent dance sounds on week nights, a broader spectrum at weekends. ✆ Rua dos Poiais de São Bento 37 • Map F4

7 Clube do Mercado
This bar and club is now crucial to the Lisbon scene. It has an ambitious programme covering hip-hop, funk, soul, drum 'n' bass and

Buddha Lx

Bairro Alto has Lisbon's greatest concentration of small bars (see p76) more. On Thursday nights there is live music, at weekends there are DJ sets, and Tuesdays see parties hosted by Erasmus Lisboa European exchange students. ✆ *Rua das Taipas 8 • Map K2*

Bar do Rio
What is arguably Lisbon's grooviest club occupies certainly the most successful warehouse conversion along the quays. The space isn't huge, the crowd is far from pimply, and the atmosphere is slightly glamorous yet relaxed, enhanced by mellow house and funky sounds. ✆ *Armazém A, Porta 7, Cais do Sodré • Map K6*

Op Art

Op Art
A beacon of taste and good music in the Docas area, Op Art is a small glass pavilion by the river, used as a café-restaurant during the day and a discerning DJ bar throughout the night. Late evenings and dawns can be magical. ✆ *Doca de Santo Amaro • Map D6*

Jamaica
In a fading red-light district and much beloved among seekers of old Lisbon, Jamaica caters broadly to nostalgia and the need to dance. The crowd is mixed – hip young things and greying types who can't work out the current musical vibe – and the mood easy. Tuesday nights are dedicated to reggae; others offer a cocktail of styles. ✆ *Rua Nova de Carvalho 6–8 • Map K6*

Fado Venues

Clube de Fado
This essential Alfama venue is owned by *guitarrista* Mário Pacheco, who gives exposure to new stars. ✆ *Rua de São João da Praça • 21 885 27 04*

Parreirinha de Alfama
A traditional venue owned by the famous Argentina Santos. ✆ *Beco do Espírito Santo 1 • 21 886 82 09*

Senhor Vinho
Quality and style, rather than grit, characterize the singing at this expensive *fado* restaurant. ✆ *Rua do Meio à Lapa 18 • 21 397 26 81*

Timpanas
Timpanas offers a superb dinner show with first-class *fado*. ✆ *Rua Gilberto Rola 24 • 21 390 66 55*

Tasca do Chico
Gritty *fado vadio*: amateur impromptu performances. ✆ *Rua Diário de Notícias 39 • 965 059 670*

Nónó
This *fado vadio* place has relatively inexpensive food. ✆ *Rua do Norte 47 • 21 342 99 89*

Os Ferreiras
A small grill restaurant and a serious *fado* venue. ✆ *Rua de São Lázaro 150 • 21 885 08 51*

Associação Concentração Musical de 24 de Agosto
For a taste of real Lisbon culture, stay late at this friendly venue. ✆ *Travessa do Oleiro 13*

Casa de Linhares
The *fado* side of a *bacalhau* restaurant. ✆ *Beco dos Armazéns do Linho 2 • 21 886 50 88*

O Faia
One of Bairro Alto's larger *fado* venues. Good music, expensive food. ✆ *Rua da Barroca 54 • 21 342 67 42*

Fado (literally "Fate") is Lisbon's own music, with a tradition going back over 150 years. Museu do Fado (see p58) is a good place to start.

Left **Bica do Sapato** Right **A Travessa**

🔟 Restaurants

1 Eleven
A Modernist window box at the top of Parque Eduardo VII is the setting for Lisbon's most sophisticated contemporary restaurant. Joachim Koerper and his team have already bagged a Michelin star for the meticulously prepared food; he is aiming for a second. 🛇 *Rua Marquês da Fronteira, Jardim Amália Rodrigues • Map E2 • 21 386 22 11 • Closed Sun • €€€€€*

2 Bica do Sapato
Size and experience keep Bica do Sapato ahead of newer contemporary restaurants in Lisbon. Downstairs there is a bar and a dining room; upstairs a sushi restaurant. Fish is the thing here – but not the usual grilled versions served with potatoes. 🛇 *Avenida Infante Dom Henrique/Cais da Pedra, Armazém B • Map R3 • 21 881 03 20 • Closed Sun & Mon L • €€€€*

3 Terreiro do Paço
The *raison d'être* of this restaurant is to showcase the food and produce of Portugal – not by laying on extravagant buffets or selling over-packaged samples, but by serving up imaginative versions of classic Portuguese dishes, all made with certified Portuguese ingredients, and accompanied by Portuguese wines. 🛇 *Lisboa Welcome Center, Praça do Comércio • Map M6 • 21 031 28 50 • €€€€€*

4 Real Fábrica
Justa and António Nobre already have their place in the annals of Portuguese gastronomy assured for their Nobre restaurant in Ajuda. At this first-floor place near Largo do Rato, you can try Justa's crab soup, served in the shell, or her dishes based on pheasant or grouper. 🛇 *Rua da Escola Politécnica 275 • Map F3 • 21 385 20 90 • Closed Sun • €€€€*

5 A Travessa
In the grand surroundings of an old convent (shared with a puppet museum and private residents) is this welcoming restaurant that feels like it could be in a provincial town. The food, though, is cosmopolitan, successfully mixing Portuguese, Belgian and French influences to gourmet effect. 🛇 *Travessa do Convento das Bernardas 12 • Map F5 • 21 390 20 34 • Closed Sat L, Sun & Mon L • €€€€*

6 Casa do Alentejo
Overlooking a wonderful Moorish-style interior courtyard, this "embassy of the Alentejo region" is one of Lisbon's most memorable dining locations. Stick to soups, rice dishes or fish and you won't forget the food either. 🛇 *Rua das Portas de Santo Antão 58 (upstairs) • Map L2 • 21 340 51 40 • €€*

Eleven

➡ *For tips on eating out* See **p110**

7 Tavares
A cavern of gilt, stucco, and heavy mirrors, Tavares, opened in 1784, claims to be Lisbon's oldest restaurant; the impressive decor, though, is early 20th-century. The fortunes of this restaurant have fluctuated, but with a French chef at the helm, it appears as enduring as ever. *Rua da Misericórdia 37 • Map L4 • 21 342 11 12 • Closed Sun & Mon • €€€€€*

Tavares

8 Vírgula
Vírgula offers superb river views and the relative rarity of Portuguese new-wave cuisine. *Rua do Cintura do Porto 16, Armazém B • Map J6 • 21 343 20 02 • Closed Sun • €€€€*

9 La Moneda
Modern food in a modern setting was La Moneda's aim. Prices have risen, along with culinary ambitions, but the informality makes it great for a social meal. *Rua da Moeda 1C • Map J5 • 21 390 80 12 • Closed Sun • €€€*

10 Stop do Bairro
This Campo de Ourique place is sought out for its generous portions, non-formulaic cooking, friendly service, good wine list and outdoor tables. Indoors, it's bright, crowded, loud and smoky. *Rua Tenente Ferreira Durão 55A • Map E3 • 21 388 88 56 • Closed Mon • €€*

Top 10 Cafés and *Pastelarias*

1 Antiga Confeitaria de Belém
The birthplace of the original *pastel de nata* is a site of pilgrimage *(see p86)*.

2 Confeitaria Nacional
Here you will spot many rotund ladies bearing cardboard boxes tied with string – a sure sign of quality *(see p68)*.

3 Bénard
For cakes, this is a better option than the crowded A Brasileira next door *(see p75)*.

4 Casa Suiça
Classy but affordable café with outdoor tables on both Rossio and Praça da Figueira *(see p68)*.

5 Leitaria Caneças
This quality bakery and pastry shop near the British Bar *(see p68)* is also a café. *Rua Bernardino Costa 36*

6 Café Mexicana
A classic Lisbon café-restaurant and social club – big and busy *(see p95)*.

7 Pastelaria Versailles
Dream your way back to a time before fast food in this unreformed relic of old Lisbon *(see p95)*.

8 Panificação Mecânica
Its name taken from its early use of baking machinery, this bakery and pastry shop is an Art-Nouveau jewel. *Rua Silva Carvalho 209–25*

9 Pau de Canela
This café has a terrace on the small but sweet Praça das Flores. Children can play safely nearby. *Praça das Flores 27*

10 O Chá da Lapa
Experience a Lisbon tea salon – for the cakes, the atmosphere and the smart Lapa ladies. *Rua do Olival 8–10*

For more restaurant listings, and a guide to restaurant price bands See pp61, 69, 77, 85, 89, 95 and 103

Left **Buying fish at Rua de São Pedro fish market** Right **Pastéis de Nata**

🔟 Culinary Highlights

1 Arroz de Marisco
This king of Portuguese rice dishes is more moist than a paella and less sticky than a risotto. It should contain shellfish, in the shell for flavour (lobster claws, pieces of spider crab, prawns, clams and cockles), as well as a streak of chilli and a liberal sprinkling of fresh coriander. Many restaurants cook it once a week and serve it in enormous portions.

2 Açorda
Originally a poor man's soup from the Alentejo, Açorda was simply water flavoured with garlic and oil, and thickened with a slice of yesterday's bread and an egg. Most restaurants now do a more sophisticated **Açorda de Marisco** version in which the soup is a sort of purée, studded with seafood (*marisco*) or served with small fillets of deep-fried fish. Pap'Açorda *(see p77)* makes one of the best.

3 Bacalhau
Foreign visitors may find it strange that the Portuguese have such a passion for salted dried cod, fished in distant seas, when they have such a delectable fresh selection much closer at hand. The explanation involves history, economics, Salazar *(see p31)* and habit. Small croquettes of

bacalhau and mashed potatoes, *pastéis de bacalhau*, are a good introduction; then you are ready to sample some of the remaining 364 ways of preparing *bacalhau*.

4 Frango à Piri-piri
Many a visitor's fondest food memory of Portugal, this is simply grilled chicken served with chilli oil (*piri-piri* is the Portuguese-African term for chilli). The simplicity is deceptive, though: in the best versions of the dish, the chicken has been treated to a thorough marinade before grilling.

5 Ameijoas à Bulhão Pato
All truly great dishes combine just a few flavours, with a minimum of fuss. This one is a prime example: *ameijoa* clams cooked briefly in their own juices, olive oil and plenty of whole, crushed garlic cloves, and served with coriander and lemon wedges. Bread is the only accompaniment.

6 Fresh Fish
Go to a good fishmonger and you will be presented with an encyclopedic choice of fish, from bass and bream to John Dory, eel, skate and parrot fish. Good restaurants for sampling some of these include Bica do Sapato *(see p44)* and Porto de Santa Maria *(see p103)*.

7 Smoked and Cured Ham and Meats

Presunto is the Portuguese name for cured ham. Usually dried in salt, it is sometimes also smoked, and often rolled in bright orange paprika powder. *Enchidos* is the collective term for a bewildering but rewarding array of sausages and salamis. These are often heavily smoked and spiced.

8 Pastéis de Nata

Small custard tarts are a staple of Lisbon cafés, taken on the run with a piercing *bica*, the city's term for espresso. Sometimes sprinkled with cinnamon and always reassuringly gooey, they are made to the original recipe at the Antiga Confeitaria in Belém *(see p86)*. All others are imitations, so they say.

9 Soups

Soup in Portugal is the traditional meal opener, and is often made with vegetables (though the stock will almost invariably be chicken, with bits of smoked sausage, *chouriço*, added as spice). The most famous is *caldo verde*, made with the kale that grows in the north – shredded in a special machine – and potato, and spiced with *chouriço*. One of the richest is *sopa da pedra* (stone soup), containing a little bit of everything (and a stone, according to the legend).

10 Picanha

Picanha was originally a Brazilian cut of rump steak, grilled whole and served in thin slices with black-bean stew and other accompaniments. However, it has become so popular that it is now made with local cuts of beef and served in many non-Brazilian restaurants. It is very flavourful, if not always tender meat.

Top 10 Portuguese Wines

1 Quinta do Vale
One of the best modern reds is made with grapes from the vineyards far up the Douro valley that used to supply the legendary Barca Velha.

2 Niepoort
Originally Dutch, this family-owned port shipper has emerged as one of the great innovators in table wines.

3 Quinta do Crasto
This is a quality producer of modern Douro wine and good-value port, particularly the unfiltered LBVs.

4 Ferreira
A Douro institution, home of Barca Velha and of later greats such as Quinta da Leda.

5 Vallado
A reliable producer of Douro reds in the muscular category, Vallado is superb value and a Douro vanguard.

6 Quinta da Pellada
One of the best Dão producers of the day makes wines that are more elegant than many from the Douro.

7 Quinta do Monte d'Oiro
This Estremadura producer shows the region is capable of great wines – made mainly from French grapes.

8 Tapada de Coelheiros
Some of the region's most concentrated reds come from this small Alentejo wine maker.

9 Esporão
One of the success stories of the Alentejo makes reds and whites, varietals and blends, of reliably high quality.

10 João Portugal Ramos
This company is purveyor of some of the most popular modern Portuguese wines.

A good place to sample Portuguese wine is Enoteca **See p95**

Left **Sandy beach and promenade along the bay of Estoril** Right **Guincho beach**

Beaches

Caparica North
The northern stretch of the Caparica coast is the busiest, with Caparica town, plus mid-range hotels, holiday homes, camp sites and restaurants.

Caparica Centre
Heading south, the beach gets less busy, but has fewer amenities. From late spring to early autumn the Transpraia train runs from Caparica town to Fonte da Telha, stopping at bars and restaurants en route. The beach at Fonte da Telha is busy and family-oriented. Many bars are closed out of season.

Caparica Centre

Carcavelos
The broadest and longest beach along the Estoril coast is far enough from Lisbon for clean water and yet close enough for an afternoon outing. Though its reputation suffered after a single, much-publicized "robbery stampede" in 2005, in which groups of youths on the beach

Carcavelos

suddenly grabbed valuables from their neighbours, security has as a result been stepped up. Carcavelos is still extremely pleasant out of season.

Lagoa de Albufeira and Meco
The southern half of the Caparica coast is accessible only by driving towards Sesimbra – or after a very long walk along the beach. Lagoa de Albufeira, a lagoon, is popular for wind-surfing. Meco, further south, is backed by a village with restaurants and bars.

Estoril and Cascais
These beaches get crowded as they are mostly short and narrow. Still, the promenade that runs just above them, all the way from Estoril to Cascais, is full of relaxed bars and eateries, where you can also take the sun.

Guincho
Guincho can provide an eyeful of sand on a windy day, but experienced surfers love it and it gives the fullest taste of nature of all the beaches along the Estoril coast. Beyond the built-up outskirts of Cascais, and with the Sintra hills as a backdrop, it is a beautiful spot with magnificent beaches and draws the crowds on summer weekends. To avoid parking

hassles, rent a bicycle in Cascais and ride out on the track that runs alongside the spectacular coast road.

7 Ursa

Not marked on maps and requiring a steep descent along narrow paths, Ursa is one of the most secluded beaches in the region. Surrounded by towering cliffs like giants seated in the surf, there are no amenities and anything beyond a short swim near the beach is ill advised. The beach is reached along the road to Cabo da Roca, where there is a small sign marked Ursa. Park your car out of sight of the main road (don't leave any valuables in it) and head down the path.

Adraga

8 Adraga

Beyond Cabo da Roca, this pretty beach is reached via Almoçageme, off the Sintra road. The area is affected by Sintra's cooler climate. The single restaurant is excellent.

9 Grande

With the longest unbroken stretch of sand in the area, Grande is popular with surfers and body boarders. There are bars and restaurants, and one hotel.

10 Das Maçãs

"Apple Beach" is one of the most family-friendly along the Sintra-Colares coast. Lots of good seafood restaurants are to be found nearby.

Top 10 Outdoor Activities

1 Walking

For dirt rather than cobbles underfoot, head for Sintra, Arrábida or the Tejo estuary.

2 Cycling

Though rare in Lisbon, bikes can be rented in Cascais and Parque das Nações.

3 Board Sports

Surfing and body-boarding are big along the Estoril and Sintra coasts, as is kite surfing on the Caparica coast.

4 Fishing

Fishermen seem to be all along the river and beaches. There are good spots near Cascais, where boats are used.

5 Bird-watching

The Tagus marshlands beyond Alcochete and the Tróia peninsula are rich in bird life at almost all times of year.

6 Sailing

There are sailing schools in Parque das Nações, Belém and along the Estoril coast. Renting larger craft is possible.

7 Horse Riding

There are a number of equestre or hípico clubs around Cascais and Sintra, and at Belas nearer Lisbon.

8 Jogging

The western river front is reasonable jogging territory, as is Parque Eduardo VII. Monsanto and the Guincho coast are other options.

9 Mountain Biking

Lisbon hosts a small but hotly contested downhill bike race each May, the Lisbon Downtown. For country tracks, head to Sintra or Arrábida.

10 Roller Skating

Parque das Nações, the Alcântara docks and Belém all have areas suited to skating.

Surf forecasts for Portugal can be found on www.surf-forecast.com

Left **Oceanário** Right **Monsanto**

🔟 Activities for Children

1 Monsanto
"Lisbon's lungs" is an unruly pine wood on the city's western fringes. The Parque Recreativo do Alto da Serafina and Parque Infantil do Alvito are fenced-off, well-equipped play parks (see p83). ◈ Map D2

2 Jardim Zoológico
Lisbon's zoo has features that are particularly popular with children. These include a train and an open-air cable car, which allows you to view many of the enclosures from above. Other

Sea Lion at Lisbon Zoo

attractions include an aquatic show with dolphins and sea lions, and a good reptile house. ◈ Praça Marechal Humberto Delgado • Map D1 • Mar–Sep: 10am–8pm daily; Oct–Feb: 10am–6pm daily (last adm 1 hr 15 mins before closing) • Adm charge

3 Oceanário
Opened for the 1998 Lisbon Expo, the Oceanarium remains the biggest single attraction in Parque das Nações. The second-

Knowledge Pavilion – Ciência Viva

largest aquarium in the world, it holds an impressive array of species (see pp16–17).

4 Knowledge Pavilion – Ciência Viva
This hands-on science museum has vast halls full of intriguing gadgetry to illustrate important fundamental laws of nature as well as more exotic phenomena. Downstairs, the youngest visitors get the chance to don hard hats and help build the Unfinished House (see pp16–17).

5 Quinta Pedagógica
This city farm gives children the chance to handle baby animals and learn about rural activities and crafts. ◈ Rua Cidade de Lobito • Map C1 • Jun–Sep: 9am–6pm Tue–Fri, 11am–6pm Sat & Sun; Oct–May: 9am–5:30pm Tue–Fri, 11am–5:30pm Sat & Sun

6 Colombo
Lisbon's mega-mall has a Funcenter on the top floor, with slot machines, games and rides, plus a bowling alley. ◈ Avenida Lusíada • Map B2 • Noon–midnight daily

7 Roller Skating, Ice Skating and Skateboarding
There are several places in Lisbon with ramps and rinks for feet with wheels. Two of the best are on Avenida Brasília by the Alcântara Docks, and by the Vasco da Gam

Quinta Pedagógica

tower in Parque das Nações. In winter, there is an outdoor ice rink near Largo de Santos.

Swimming Pools

8 Many hotels have outdoor pools, but for those without, the Clube Nacional de Natação has a recently renovated complex at Rua de São Bento 209, with indoor and outdoor pools. An alternative is Olaias Clube at Rua Robalo Gouveia in east Lisbon.

Beaches

9 Beaches are great places for children, but the Atlantic is not the safest water for young ones to play in. Low tide is a good time for building sand castles and wallowing in pools left by the receding sea. Some of the beaches along the Estoril coast (see p48) are more protected; otherwise head for Portinho de Arrábida or Tróia (see p52).

Museu de Ciência

10 Housed in the grand setting of the old Polytechnic, this science museum by the Jardim Botânico (see p80) has an ageing but engaging hands-on exhibit illustrating basic principles of physics.
◆ Rua da Escola Politécnica 58 • Map J2
Open 10am–5pm Tue–Fri, 11am–6pm Sat & Sun • Adm charge

Top 10 Family-friendly Restaurants

Casanova

1 A popular quay-side pizzeria with a safe veranda; kids can even watch the chef (see p61).

31 da Armada

2 Plus points at this place include the traffic-free square and friendly staff. ◆ Praça da Armada 31 • 21 397 63 30

Ton Xin

3 A vast Chinese restaurant, with plenty of running space inside and out (see p85).

Café Buenos Aires

4 The steps outside are traffic free; inside, the vibe is accommodating (see p77).

Psi

5 The location, in a garden with ponds, adds to parents' relaxation; the no-alcohol policy may not (see p95).

Papagaio da Serafina

6 A pavilion-style restaurant with an ambitious menu in Monsanto's best children's park. ◆ Parque Recreativo do Alto da Serafina • 21 774 28 88

Jardim dos Sentidos

7 Here vegetarian food is served in a lovely space with an interior garden. ◆ Rua da Mãe d'Água 3 • 21 342 36 70

Restaurants at Doca de Santo Amaro

8 Facing a marina, these eateries have outdoor tables and attract families. ◆ Doca de Santo Amaro

Restaurants in Parque das Nações

9 Choices range from food courts to riverside terraces; steak houses to floating restaurants. ◆ Parque das Nações

Restaurants along Rua Vieira Portuense

10 This short street of outdoor restaurants in Belém overlooks the Jardim de Belém (see p85).

Original-language screenings of children's films are listed as v.o., for versão original.

Left **Crenellated Óbidos** Right **Spring flowers by the saltpans of the Tejo estuary near Alcochete**

Excursions

Sintra hills
The romantic beauty of Sintra *(see pp26–7)* and its palaces, the crumbling walls veiled with moss, the views, the winding roads under dense canopies of leaves, the smell of the air and the thoughts evoked make Sintra and its hills a magical world.

Serra da Arrábida
This limestone massif, about 40 minutes south of Lisbon by car, provides in its vegetation and calm, blue-green waters Portugal's most Mediterranean scenery. It also has dramatic cliffs. Head for Portinho da Arrábida, and stop often as you get close.

Palmela and Azeitão
The main sight in Palmela is the hill-top castle, now an elegant *pousada* open to passing visitors. Vila Fresca de Azeitão and Vila Nogueira de Azeitão are neighbouring towns at the heart of the Palmela wine country.

Aerial view of Palmela's castle

Setúbal and Tróia
The port town of Setúbal is prosaic, but it is home to the Igreja de Jesus, the first and perhaps most distinctive example of the Manueline style. People and cars are ferried across the mouth of the Sado river to the finger-like peninsula of Tróia, with excellent, undeveloped beaches extending south and a rich bird life on its estuary side.

Alcácer do Sal
The name itself is a bilingual history lesson, mixing the Arabic for castle and the Portuguese for salt. The town's once-Moorish castle is now a *pousada*, while the salt trade that dates back two millennia now plays a smaller role than rice-growing.

Tejo Estuary
The Tejo estuary is easily accessible from Lisbon via the town of Alcochete, just across the Vasco da Gama bridge. From here you can venture into the *lezíria* marshlands by car or on foot. This area is one of Europe's ten most important staging sites for migrating water birds, including flamingo, black-tailed godwit and avocet.

Mafra
Mafra is home to an extravagant palace and monastery built for Dom João V, Portugal's 18th-century monarch with a weakness for excesses of all kinds. The almost pyramidal

 Driving in Portugal requires composure and vigilance. Ignore provocations by other drivers.

Library at Mafra's palace

proportions of its construction are entertainingly detailed in José Saramago's novel *Balthazar and Blimunda*. The hunting grounds are now used for a wolf conservation project.

8 Óbidos

Óbidos is arguably the most picturesque town in Portugal, contained within the walls of a 14th-century castle and filled with whitewashed houses whose edges are painted ochre or blue and whose windows wear lace curtains and geraniums in pots. The town was the wedding gift of Dom Dinis to his queen, Isabel of Aragon, in 1282.

9 Vila Franca de Xira

A centre for bullfighting, this town hosts the *Festa do Colete Encarnado* in July every year, a raucous and showy festival that includes bull-running. A similar festival, the *Feira do Outubro*, is held in October.

10 Ribatejo Wine Route

Some of the best wine producers in the Ribatejo region are clustered on the left bank of the Tejo, just north of Vila Franca de Xira, particularly between the towns of Almeirim and Alpiarça. Most welcome visitors. Seek out Quinta do Casal Branco, Quinta da Alorna, Fiuza & Bright and Quinta da Lagoalva de Cima.

Top 10 Beauty Spots

1 Guincho Coast
Cars drive very slowly – a rare thing in Portugal – along this scenic coast road, to take in the natural beauty.

2 Castelo dos Mouros
The steeply stepped walls of this attractive old castle offer fabulous views.

3 Penedo
This village on the high road from Sintra to the coast is misty and romantic in winter and a cool refuge in summer.

4 Peninha
A vantage point for views of Europe's western edge and a small group of buildings with an intriguing history *(see p102)*.

5 Ursa
This beach is worth visiting out of season, and without swimming gear, for the sheer beauty of the place *(see p49)*.

6 Monserrate
The gardens and palace-pavilion of Monserrate, with a history of English gardeners and visitors, remain popular.

7 Portinho da Arrábida
One of the most protected beaches along the entire western seaboard looks as if it belongs in Croatia or Turkey.

8 Pancas and Around
If you prefer flat expanses with huge skies and endless views, head for this hamlet just northeast of Alcochete, on the edge of the *lezíria*.

9 Cabo Espichel
The cliff-top southwestern-most point of the Setúbal peninsula is in some ways more attractive than the more illustrious Cabo da Roca.

10 Bucelas and Beyond
Head here for a taste of rolling inland Estremadura – and some great white wine.

AROUND LISBON

LISBON'S TOP 10

Left **Museu do Teatro Romano** Right **Largo das Portas do Sol**

Alfama, Castelo & the East

LFAMA'S ARABIC-SOUNDING NAME AND ANTHILL LAYOUT *are testament to its past as an important district of Moorish Lisbon – or, more likely, originally two districts: one on the riverside of fishermen and sea folk, and one on the hillside of higher society. No buildings survive from this era, but Alfama suffered little damage in the 1755 earthquake, so its medieval street plan has remained intact. And that is what makes it such a joy to explore, without the interference of traffic. The Castelo neighbourhood at the top adjoins the higher hill district of Graça and also Mouraria, a less touristic area. To the south and east, Alfama descends to the river.*

Castelo de São Jorge

🔟 Sights

1. Castelo de São Jorge
2. Museu do Teatro Romano
3. Sé Catedral
4. Largo das Portas do Sol
5. Largo de São Miguel
6. Museu do Fado
7. Santo Estêvão
8. Igreja de Santa Engrácia/ Panteão Nacional
9. Fundação Ricardo do Espírito Santo Silva
10. Museu Nacional do Azulejo

Preceding pages **Spiral staircase descending into initiation well, Quinta da Regaleira, Sintra**

1 Castelo de São Jorge
The castle that crowns Alfama was the heart of the city in the Moorish era, and the site goes back to Phoenician times at least. The picturesque residential area within the castle's outer walls is also called Castelo (see pp8–9).

2 Museu do Teatro Romano
A Roman amphitheatre from the 1st century BC lurks beneath the buildings just above the Sé. Not a lot has yet been excavated, but it seems to have been large, seating maybe 5,000. Excavations continue, so visitors get an insight into archeological work. ⊗ Pátio do Aljube 5 • Map N4 • 21 882 03 20 • Open 10am–1pm, 2–6pm Tue–Sun

3 Sé Catedral
The English crusader Gilbert of Hastings, Lisbon's first bishop, oversaw the construction of the city's cathedral in the mid-12th century. The site was previously occupied by a mosque, parts of which have been excavated in the cloister (see pp12–13).

4 Largo das Portas do Sol
When the 28 tram gets to the top of the hill beyond the Sé, it squeezes between two buildings

A street in the area of São Miguel

in what used to be the Moorish-era city walls. From here there is one of the best views of Alfama and the river. Backtrack past the Santa Luzia church, where the tram squeezed by, and you reach the Miradouro de Santa Luzia, one of the city's official viewpoints (see p36). Across the street are two access routes to the castle. There are several outdoor cafés in the area. ⊗ Map P4

5 Largo de São Miguel
You can reach this square, in the heart of Alfama, via steps from Largo das Portas do Sol: walk down next to Santa Luzia church and bear left after the first corner. This is the essence of Alfama: narrow alleys that white-haired residents use as gardens, grills the size of shoe-boxes with sardines smoking, patios, archways and twisting stairs. And the blissful absence of cars lets children play everywhere. Largo de São Miguel is at the centre of the huge party thrown to honour St Anthony, Lisbon's principal patron saint, on 12 June every year. ⊗ Map P4

Sé Catedral

Museu do Fado

Also called the Casa do Fado e da Guitarra Portuguesa, this is dedicated to Lisbon's most famous musical genre and to the mandolin-shaped Portuguese "guitar". The instrument, whose strings are in pairs, combines with the singer's soaring tremolos to give Fado – often compared with the Blues – its unique sound. The museum is surprisingly recent, but its life-size replica of a Fado venue – complete with models of singer, musicians, staff and customers – has an old-fashioned feeling to it. There is an outdoor café, and concerts are held from time to time.

- Largo do Chafariz de Dentro 1
- 21 882 3470 • 10am–6pm Tue–Sun
- Adm charge

Santo Estevão

The small esplanade in front of the Santo Estevão church is one of the area's best viewing

Marble interior, Igreja de Santa Engrácia

points. Access is easy, if steep, from Largo do Chafariz do Dentro, at the foot of Alfama, where you will find one of the city's oldest public fountains (as well as the Fado Museum, so you can easily combine a visit to both). Just head up Rua dos Remédios until you see steps on your left called Escadas de Santo Estevão; climb them and you're there. ⬡ Map Q4

Igreja de Santa Engrácia/Panteão Nacional

The soaring dome of Santa Engrácia is a landmark on Lisbon's low eastern skyline, but when you approach it on foot it seems to duck out of view at every turn. This serves to remind you that the dome was added as recently as 1966, 284 years after the construction of the church began. This in turn has enriched the Portuguese language with a saying that translates as "a job like Santa Engrácia", for any interminable project. Built on a Greek cross plan with rounded arms, the church has similarities to St Peter's Basilica in Rome,

---

Saint Anthony of the Sardines

The celebration of St Anthony, on 12 June, falls close to the feast-days of other saints (São João and São Pedro, or John and Peter) and has been turned into a two-week party known as the *Festas dos Santos Populares*. In fact, the city has gone one up on this and declared the whole month *Festas da Cidade*, with a full programme of events. Concerts, shows, processions and ceremonies aside, the real party is in Largo de São Miguel in Alfama, on the night of 12 June. Tables are set up everywhere, grills are fired up and loaded with sardines covered in coarse salt, the wine and beer flow freely, bands play, children run riot, lovers woo and grannies gossip. For a taste of sardines in the right setting, and of good-natured Lisbon neighbourliness, there's no better occasion.

although Santa Engrácia is even-sided. The airy, marble-clad interior serves as the National Pantheon *(see p32)*.

9 Fundação Ricardo do Espírito Santo Silva

Named after the banker who bequeathed a 17th-century Alfama palace filled with his collections of decorative arts, this foundation's museum displays an extensive collection of Portuguese, French and English furniture in period settings. Next door are workshops for traditional crafts such as cabinet-making, gilding and bookbinding. The foundation also runs two schools of arts and crafts, in other locations. ✎ *Largo das Portas do Sol 2 • Map P4 • 21 888 1991 • 10am–5pm daily • Adm charge*

10 Museu Nacional do Azulejo

Beyond Alfama, in the eastern Xabregas district, is the Tile Museum, housed in a stunning former 16th-century convent with an elaborately decorated church. Highlights include a small Manueline cloister, a 23-m (75-ft) panel of painted tiles showing Lisbon in the 1740s, and extensive collections of Moorish and Portuguese tiles. The café-restaurant is a pleasant place to take a break *(see pp20–21)*.

Museu Nacional do Azulejo

Alfama Wandering

Morning

Alfama is really the sort of place to wander around with an open mind rather than an open book. Like most labyrinthine medieval quarters it is actually quite small, but it seems large to the first-time visitor. Here are a few pointers, to get you on your way to losing your way. The street that begins on the right side of the Sé, briefly called **Cruzes da Sé** and then **Rua de São João da Praça**, is a good point of entry. There are also some worthwhile cafés and bars along here, including **Pois** and **Ondajazz** Bar *(see p60)*. Don't turn right off this street, or you'll be led down and out of the maze. Instead, keep going and follow it round, and you'll eventually reach **Rua de São Pedro**, which leads down to **Largo do Chafariz de Dentro**, where there's a good choice of restaurants for lunch.

Afternoon

To return to the maze, head back up Rua de São Pedro and do a near 180-degree turn at the top to reach **Igreja de São Miguel**. Now you are into *beco* (alley) territory. Follow left turns by right turns and you should be able to weave your way to **Santo Estêvão**. Should thirst overcome you, head down the steps to **Mestre André** *(see p61)*. A brisk walk up Rua dos Remedios and then along Rua do Paraíso will get you to **Campo de Santa Clara** and, if it's Tuesday or Saturday, the **Feira da Ladra** *(see p41)*. If it's not, stroll down to the riverside row of converted ware-houses at **Santa Apolónia** for another kind of shopping experience *(see pp60–61)*.

Left **Chapitô** Right **Pois, Café**

Bars and Cafés

Cerca Moura
Right by the Portas do Sol viewpoint is this popular, largely outdoor bar and café. Indoors, it's a cosy cubbyhole inside what was once Moorish Lisbon's town walls. ◈ *Largo das Portas do Sol 4 • Map P4*

Bar das Imagens
The outdoor tables have a great view at sunset but stand on a slight incline; people have been known to slide off their chairs before they've finished their first drink. The restaurant inside is strong on starters. ◈ *Calçada Marquês de Tancos 1 • Map N4*

Chapitô
This large, friendly bar, café and restaurant offers a variety of seating areas and superb views. The complex is owned by a school of performing arts. ◈ *Costa do Castelo 7 • Map N4*

Santiago Alquimista
Set in the spacious base-ment of a drama school, this bar is at the vanguard of Lisbon's musical and multicultural scene. ◈ *Rua de Santiago 19 • Map P4*

Pois, Café
This living-room-style café, with a cool but relaxed vibe, was a first in Lisbon when it was opened by its Austrian owners. *Pois* is a much-used Portuguese word that evidently sounded quaint to Austrian ears. ◈ *Rua de São João da Praça 93–5 • Map P5*

Ondajazz Bar
The French team behind this pleasant bar lays on live jazz and other cool musical choices in this vaulted former coffee warehouse. ◈ *Arco de Jesus 7 • Map P5*

Esplanada da Igreja da Graça
One of Lisbon's best café-table views is to be had from the esplanade by the vast Graça church *(see p33)*. Particularly good on sunny late afternoons, it is less attractive after sunset. ◈ *Largo da Graça • Map P2*

Deli Delux
This is a well-stocked deli with a café at the back and a small terrace. Its weekend brunches are great, but come early to avoid having to wait for a table – though there are plenty of shops to distract you if you do. ◈ *Avenida Infante Dom Henrique/Cais da Pedra, Armazém B, Loja 8 • Map R3*

Cefalópode
Drop in to this laid-back bar on the way up to the castle for live music at weekends and jam sessions, poetry readings and art exhibitions on other days. ◈ *Largo do Contador-Mor 4B • Map P4*

Última Sé
This DJ-driven bar in a narrow alley behind the Sé *(see pp12–13)* has a tiny dance floor, themed party nights and occasional live acts. ◈ *Travessa do Almargem 1 • Map N5*

Check the Agenda Cultural (see p107) for events listings at some of the bars above.

Price Categories

For a three course	**€** under €15
meal for one with half	**€€** €15–€20
a bottle of wine (or	**€€€** €20–€30
equivalent meal), taxes	**€€€€** €30–€40
and extra charges.	**€€€€€** over €40

Casa do Leão

🏆🔟 Restaurants

1 Bica do Sapato
Lisbon's most talked-about restaurant is an airy 1970s-retro space by the river, with modern food and a sushi bar upstairs. Trendy but not tediously so, it is part owned by John Malkovich *(see p44)*.

2 Casanova
Lisbon's best pizzas are served at this lively restaurant with a terrace on the quay. No bookings are taken, so arrive early to avoid a wait. ◉ *Avenida Infante Dom Henrique/Cais da Pedra, Armazém B, Loja 7 • Map R3 • 21 887 75 32 • Closed Mon L & D; Tue L • €€*

3 D'Avis
Well-prepared food from the Alentejo region is on the menu at this tavern. Try dishes of *porco preto*, flavourful free-range Iberian pig. ◉ *Rua do Grilo 96–8 • Map C2 • 21 868 13 54 • Closed Sun • €€€*

4 Casa do Leão
Housed in the remains of the original Alcáçovas castle *(see p9)* is this grand restaurant with an ambitious Portuguese menu. Sit outside, with Lisbon at your feet. ◉ *Castelo de São Jorge • Map N3 • 21 887 59 62 • Open L & D daily • €€€€*

5 Arco do Castelo
Genuine Goan restaurants like this one are now quite a rarity. Try spicy specialities like *sarapatel*, *balchão de porco* or chicken *xacuti*. ◉ *Rua Chão da Feira 25 • Map N4 • 21 887 65 98 • Closed Sun • €*

6 Faz Figura
There are wonderful views of the river from a large terrace. The recently upgraded menu includes international dishes. ◉ *Rua do Paraíso 15b • Map R3 • 21 886 89 81 • Open daily • €€€€*

7 Mercado de Santa Clara
Upstairs in an old market hall, on the square hosting a flea market every Tuesday and Saturday, this friendly place has quality Portuguese cooking. ◉ *Campo de Santa Clara • Map Q2 • 21 887 39 86 • Closed Mon • €€€*

8 Mestre André
Traditional Portuguese fare is the speciality of this informal restaurant, which is popular with Alfama's newer residents. ◉ *Calçadinha de Santo Estêvão 6 • Map Q4 • 21 887 14 87 • Open Mon–Sat D • €€*

9 Santo António de Alfama
Not as traditional as the name and location would suggest: the walls are lined with black-and-white portraits of film stars, but the food is modern Portuguese and international. ◉ *Beco de São Miguel 7 • Map P4 • 21 888 13 28 • Closed Tue • €€€*

10 Viagem de Sabores
Choose this charming old restaurant's "tastes journey" for a small but varied selection of dishes from all over the world. Strong on starters. ◉ *Rua de São João da Praça 103 • Map P5 • 21 887 01 89 • Open D daily, closed Sun • €€€*

Left **Bronze statue of King João I, Praça da Figuiera** Right **Praça do Comércio**

Baixa to Restauradores

FROM THE EARLY 16th to mid-18th centuries, Lisbon's royal palace stood on the riverbank, around today's Praça do Comércio. It was the grand entrance to Lisbon, one of the world's great cities. Then in 1755 the earth shook, the ocean rose and fires raged – and the Paço Real and most of the medieval jumble of buildings behind it were gone. The Baixa we see was built on the ruins of lower Lisbon, to a different plan, in a different style, for a new era. Today this is the ageing heart of Lisbon, challenged by depopulation, traffic, subsidence and shopping centres – but still loved and alive.

Triumphal arch, Praça Comércio, with Rua Augusta beyond

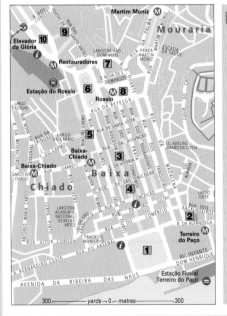

Sights

1. Praça do Comércio
2. Igreja da Conceição Velha
3. Rua Augusta
4. Núcleo Arqueológico da Rua dos Correeiros
5. Elevador de Santa Justa
6. Rossio
7. Igreja de São Domingos
8. Praça da Figueira
9. Rua das Portas de Santo Antaõ
10. Praça dos Restauradores

1 Praça do Comércio

The broad riverfront square also known as Terreiro do Paço has regained some of its stature since cars were prohibited from parking there. Surrounded on three sides by the elegant arcades of Pombal's reconstruction (see p31), and facing the river along the fourth, this is an urban space whose beauty is still crying out for a true role in the city. Dom José I, Portugal's ineffectual king at the time of the earthquake, gazes – perhaps fearfully – at the river from his horseback perch in bronze, by Machado de Castro. ⊗ Map M5

2 Igreja da Conceição Velha

Carved angel, Igreja da Conceição Velha

This was the grand 16th-century Igreja da Misericórdia before the 1755 earthquake, which destroyed everything but the Manueline portal and one interior chapel. When it opened again in 1770, it was taken over by the congregation of another Baixa church that had been irreparably damaged in the quake, the Conceição Velha. The new church was very modest, and most visitors today come to admire the detailed portal. This features a carved image of Our Lady of Mercy, her long mantle held by two angels to shelter kneeling historical figures including Dom Manuel, Pope Leo X and Dona Leonor, widow of João II and founder of the Misericórdia almshouses. ⊗ Rua da Alfândega • Map N5 • Open 8am–6pm Mon–Fri; 8am–4pm Sat; Sun for services only

3 Rua Augusta

Lisbon's longest and grandest pedestrianized street runs from one corner of Rossio through the middle of Baixa to a triumphal archway on Praça de Comércio. The arch, which commemorates the city's recovery after the 1755 earthquake, was added only in 1873. An allegorical figure of Glory stands atop it, crowning figures representing Genius and Bravery with wreaths. The gallery of national heroes below these includes the Marquis of Pombal. The side facing Rua Augusta features a large clock, much used by the shoppers who throng the street. ⊗ Map M4–5

4 Núcleo Arqueológico da Rua dos Correeiros

When a Portuguese bank (now Millennium BCP) began renovating its head office in the early 1990s, the builders' jack-hammers unearthed an-cient remnants of Roman Lisbon. A small museum was set up, and the digging goes on. So far, this has revealed parts of what appears to have been a riverside factory for making garum, the fermented fish sauce much loved by the Romans. A section of mosaic floor uncovered in a separate structure suggests other, or later uses. ⊗ Rua dos Correeiros 9 • Map M4 • Guided tours in English: Thu 3–5pm; Sat 10am–noon; book in advance

Rua Augusta

In 2010 the Design and Fashion Museum (MUDE) will reopen on Rua Augusta in Central Downtown Lisbon.

Praça Dom Pedro IV, Rossio

Elevador de Santa Justa

You may be told that this iron lift was designed by Eiffel (of the Paris tower fame), but in fact it is by Raoul Mesnier de Ponsard, his Portuguese pupil. There were once three such lifts in Lisbon's craggy cityscape, before the era of small delivery lorries. Today the Neo-Gothic lift (look at the sides of the tower) whisks lazy types and tourists from Baixa to the Carmo ruin *(see p71)*. There are photo opportunities and a scenic café *(see p68)* at the top.

Ⓢ *Rua de Santa Justa • Map M4 • Runs 7am–11pm summer, 7am–9pm winter • Bus/tram ticket*

"Only the pigeons will see it isn't him ... "

The statue atop the column in Rossio of course represents Dom Pedro IV, the king who gave his (unwanted) name to the square. But is it actually him? It's said to be of Emperor Maximilian of Mexico, whose bronze likeness was in transit in Lisbon when news came through that he had been assassinated. Since the city fathers – after much argument over the expense – had just ordered a bronze of Dom Pedro IV from the same French sculptor, agreement was reached to substitute, at cut price, the now superfluous Maximilian. This served everyone's purposes. Except Dom Pedro's, that is.

Rossio

Rossio, officially but rarely called Praça Dom Pedro IV, has been Lisbon's main square for as long as anyone can remember. Probably for longer: Roman Olisipo's hippodrome is said to have been here. Surrounded by some of the city's grandest buildings before the earthquake, it was outshone by the new Praça do Comércio after the reconstruction – but has yet to cede its position as the city's cosmopolitan, coffee-fuelled heart.
Ⓢ *Praça Dom Pedro IV • Map L3–M3*

Igreja de São Domingos

Dark and cavernous, the São Domingos church is not much visited by tourists, despite its long history. As a result, it is a good place for quiet reflection, whatever one's creed *(see p32)*.

Praça da Figueira

After the earthquake, even as the rubble of the vast Hospital Real de Todos-os-Santos was being cleared, an open-air market was set up in what is now Praça da Figueira. It became the city's main vegetable market, and eventually was roofed with iron pavilions and cupolas. Praça da Figueira joined next-door Rossio as Lisbon's bustling centre, scene of raucous Santo António celebrations in mid-June. Sadly, it is today a bleak shadow of its former self, serving as the vented lid of an underground car park, forlornly bestridden by an equestrian Dom João I looking for action. However, there are broad, shaded café esplanades along one side, and the square looks quite attractive when viewed from up on the castle ramparts.
Ⓢ *Map M3*

9 Rua das Portas de Santo Antão

This long, partly pedestrianized street has food for everyone. The legendary Gambrinus restaurant is next door to the tiny Ginjinha Sem Rival bar, and between these extremes is a rash of seafood restaurants with outdoor seating, plus the atmospheric Casa do Alentejo, the cheerful Bomjardim, and the inimitable Solmar *(see pp68–9)*. ◈ Map L2

10 Praça dos Restauradores

This plaza and its monument were built when the old Passeio Público was turned into Avenida da Liberdade in the 1870s. It commemorates the restoration of the Portuguese monarchy in 1640. The obelisk is engraved with important dates from the restoration campaign, and is flanked by statues representing the Spirit of Independence and Victory. The surrounding square is dominated by traffic; shops, cafés, kiosks and restaurants cluster in its lower corners. ◈ Map L2

Monument to the Restoration, Praça dos Restauradores

A Stroll through Baixa

Morning

🕐 Begin at the river's edge in **Praça do Comércio**, where the old palace steps can still be seen. Cross the street at the right-hand corner of the square and head up under the arcades. Turning right on Rua da Alfândega, take in the Manueline portal of **Igreja da Conceição Velha**. You can stop for coffee next door to the church at **Com Alma Caffé** *(see p68)*. Then head up Rua da Madalena, where you can drop into the **Conserveira de Lisboa** *(see p66)* if you happen to fancy some tinned Portuguese sardines. Turn left at Largo da Madalena and descend two blocks to the narrower **Rua dos Douradoures**, haunt of Fernando Pessoa's troubled alter ego in *The Book of Disquietude*. Here you will find plenty of restaurants to choose from for lunch.

Afternoon

After lunch, work your way through Baixa's grid, zig-zagging between whatever shops catch your eye. Next stop is the top left corner of **Praça da Figueira**, and a coffee outside the back of **Casa Suiça** *(see p68)*. Then walk up **Rua Dom Antão de Almada**, past fragrant shops selling herbs and other dried goods. On your right is one of Lisbon's oldest churches, **Igreja de São Domingos** *(see p32)*. Slightly left and then straight ahead is **Rua das Portas de Santo Antão**. If you've already worked up an appetite, you couldn't be in a better street; and for a pre-prandial drink, you could do worse than duck into the tiny **Ginjinha Sem Rival** bar *(see p68)* for a morello-cherry liqueur.

Left **Teatro Nacional Dona Maria II by night** Right **Detail of arch over Rossio Station entrance**

🔟 Best of the Rest

1 Elevador do Lavra
The oldest Lisbon funicular, inaugurated in 1884, is the one most tourists miss. Connecting Restauradores with Campo de Santana, it gets you to the Torel viewpoint *(see p37)*. ◈ *Largo da Anunciada/Calçada do Lavra • Map L1*

2 Rossio Station
Built in 1892, the old central station now serves Sintra *(see pp26–7)*. The statue in a niche between the horseshoe arches is of Dom Sebastião, the boy king lost in battle in 1578. ◈ *Between Rossio and Restauradores squares • Map L3*

3 Shops in Rua do Arsenal
A whiff of an older Lisbon lives on in shops selling dried fish, from *bacalhau* (salt cod) to octopus, other dried goods, wine and some fresh produce. ◈ *Map L5*

4 Museu da Sociedade Geográfica
Visit this somewhat dusty but fascinating museum for a trip back to colonial-era Portugal. ◈ *Rua das Portas de Santo Antão 100 • Map L2 • 21 342 54 01 • Visits by appointment only*

5 Teatro Nacional Dona Maria II
The Neo-Classical building housing Portugal's national theatre was built around 1840, at the same time as Rossio was paved with its characteristic black and white cobblestones. ◈ *Praça Dom Pedro IV • Map L3 • 21 325 08 00*

6 Haberdashers in Rua da Conceição
Baixa shopkeepers are buckling under competition from shopping centres; haberdashers are among the more resilient. At this string of shops you can buy a single button or a length of lace. ◈ *Between Rua Augusta and Rua da Prata • Map M5*

7 Antiga Ervanária d'Anunciada
Herbalists have always had a strong following in Portugal. This shop claims to be the country's oldest, and sells vitamin super-cures as well as traditional dried herbs for infusions. ◈ *Largo da Anunciada 13–15 • Map L2 • 21 342 79 97*

8 Shoeshiners in Largo de São Domingos
The *engraxador* is an emblematic Lisbon figure, much stereotyped in literature and film, but his is a fading trade. The surest place to find one is outside (or inside) the Ginjinha bar *(see p68)*. Expect to pay at least €1. ◈ *Map M3*

9 Arte Rústica
This shop is well stocked with the most popular regional crafts, particularly hand-painted ceramics and embroidery. ◈ *Rua do Ouro 246–8 • Map M4 • 21 342 11 27*

10 Conserveira de Lisboa
This charming wholesaler of tinned fish, especially sardines is the kind of place that makes Baixa a living museum. ◈ *Rua dos Bacalhoeiros 34 • Map N5 • 21 887 10 58*

Left **Vitorino de Sousa (tanner)** Right **Napoleão wines**

🔟 Shops

1 Azevedo Rua
The famous hatter at the northeastern corner of Rossio has managed to stay in business for 120 years despite the vagaries of hat-wearing fashions. ✆ *Praça Dom Pedro IV 69 • Map M3 • 21 342 75 11*

2 Manuel Tavares
A tourist-oriented, but good, deli between Rossio and Praça da Figueira, where wine, cheese and ham may sometimes be tasted before purchase. ✆ *Rua da Betesga 1 • Map M3 • 21 342 42 09*

3 Napoleão
This branch of a wine-shop chain offers friendly, personalized service and a wide choice of table and fortified wines, as well as some spirits. ✆ *Rua dos Fanqueiros 70 • Map N5 • 21 887 20 42*

4 Santos Ofícios
The city's best shop for handicrafts and folk art has a selection that extends well beyond the run of the mill, particularly in terms of imaginative figures made from a variety of materials. ✆ *Rua da Madalena 87 • Map N4 • 21 887 20 31*

5 Vitorino de Sousa
The only remaining tanner's in "Tanners' Street", Vitorino de Sousa sells boots, saddles and bridles, plus other equestrian and country gear. Its leather goods are handmade to order and can be shipped. ✆ *Rua dos Correeiros 200 • Map M4 • 21 342 74 58*

6 Hospital de Bonecas
The doll's hospital is not much bigger than a doll's house, but full of perfectly healthy dolls, as well as clothes and furniture for them. Barbie is not much in evidence. Dried herbs are also sold here. ✆ *Praça da Figueira 7 • Map M3 • 21 342 85 74*

7 Pollux
Round the back of the many-floored, much-maligned Pollux department store, this shop sells excellent Portuguese stainless-steel cookware, knives and other serious cooking aids. ✆ *Rua da Madalena 251 • Map M4 • 21 881 12 00*

8 Discoteca Amália
Not a disco, but a "disc shop" specializing in traditional Portuguese music. It's not all *fado*, even if it's mostly *fado*; and *fado* isn't only Amália Rodrigues, even if it's mostly her. ✆ *Rua do Ouro 272 • Map M4 • 21 346 31 65*

9 Lisbonense
At this old-school shoe shop styles are traditional, good value and sport an inner label to remind you of Lisbon. It specializes in orthopaedic shoes. ✆ *Rua Augusta 202 • Map M4 • 21 342 67 12*

10 Joalharia Correia
This jeweller's is the place for cutting, replacing and repairing semi-precious and precious gems. The shop reflects the family's colonial African background. ✆ *Rua do Ouro 245–7 • Map M4 • 21 342 73 84*

Left **A Licorista** Centre **Com Alma Caffé** Right **Café Martinho da Arcada**

TOP 10 Bars and Cafés

1 Nicola
Rossio's premier outdoor café is well sited for people-watching. It has a venerable history and a handsome marble Art-Deco interior. Downstairs, there is a restaurant. Coffee is cheapest at the bar; most expensive outside.
⊗ *Praça Dom Pedro IV 24 • Map L3*

2 Casa Suiça
Opposite Nicola across the square, and its main competitor, Suiça has a shorter history but a longer, narrower esplanade and a wider selection of pastries and snacks. Lunch and dinner are served as well, but only indoors.
⊗ *Praça Dom Pedro IV 96–104 • Map M3*

3 Confeitaria Nacional
A Lisbon institution for a Portuguese passion: cakes and pastries. It offers a busy take-away service and café tables inside under a mirror-clad ceiling.
⊗ *Praça da Figueira 18 • Map M3*

4 A Licorista
A vaulted-brick ceiling gives this rustic bar and restaurant a rather grand frame. The next-door restaurant, O Bacalhoeiro *(see p69)*, has the same owners.
⊗ *Rua dos Sapateiros 218 • Map M4*

5 British Bar
At what was once the Taverna Inglesa, haunt of Brits from local shipping firms, the selection of beers is wider than usual. The wall clock ticks anticlockwise.
⊗ *Rua Bernardino Costa 52 • Map L6*

6 Com Alma Caffé
At this low-key modern café, music, magazines and sandwiches are as important as the coffee. Com Alma means "with soul".
⊗ *Rua da Alfândega 114 • Map N5*

7 Café Martinho da Arcada
Attractively tiled in blue and white, this bustling café serves good-value lunches at the counter. A few tables are arranged inside; there are more outside under the arcades. The restaurant next door is more famous *(see opposite)*, but this is a quintessential Lisbon location.
⊗ *Praça do Comércio 3 • Map N5*

8 Esplanada Céu de Lisboa
Climb the spiral staircase after ascending the lift from the Baixa and you will be treated to a graphic overview of downtown Lisbon. Coffee, drinks and snacks are overpriced, but would you expect otherwise? ⊗ *Top of Elevador de Santa Justa • Map M4*

9 A Ginjinha
Ginjinha is Portuguese cherry liqueur and this tiny bar serves virtually nothing else. A Ginjinha has survived for over 150 years on sheer single-mindedness.
⊗ *Largo de São Domingos 8 • Map M3*

10 O'Gilins
Lisbon's first Irish pub is still the city's best, popular with students and expats alike. There is live music at weekends.
⊗ *Rua dos Remolares 8 • Map K6*

Around Town – Baixa to Restauradores

An espresso is known in Lisbon as a bica; *a café au lait is a* meia de leite.

Price Categories

For a three course meal for one with half a bottle of wine (or equivalent meal), taxes and extra charges.

€	under €15
€€	€15–€20
€€€	€20–€30
€€€€	€30–€40
€€€€€	over €40

Casa do Alentejo

🔟 Restaurants

1 Terreiro do Paço
Bearing the original, 16th-century name of the square on which it stands, this elegant gourmet restaurant offers a fresh take on Portuguese classics. The menu features certified Portuguese produce (see p44).

2 Gambrinus
This classic Lisbon address is as famous for its seafood dishes and "rich fish soup" as it is for its high prices and endless business lunches. ✪ Rua das Portas de Santo Antão 23 • Map L2 • 21 346 52 08 • €€€€€

3 Martinho da Arcada
Once a favourite of literary figures such as Fernando Pessoa, this is a good place to eat traditional Portuguese food in the right kind of setting (though outside it is noisy). ✪ Praça do Comércio 3 • Map M5 • 218 879 259 • Closed Sun • €€€

4 O Bacalhoeiro
This cosy restaurant is named after the Portuguese trawlers that fished cod off the coast of Newfoundland, then salted it on board. Don't miss the bacalhau here. ✪ Rua dos Sapateiros 220 • Map M4 • 213 431 415 • Closed Sun • €€

5 Alfândega – Armazém dos Sabores
Light, Mediterranean-style dishes are served in a pleasant, colourful space next door to the Conceição church (see p63). ✪ Rua da Alfândega 98 • Map N5 • 218 861 683 • Closed Sat L, Sun L • €€

6 Leão d'Ouro
This cathedral-like restaurant is indeed a temple: to fish. Super-fresh specimens are on display to draw custom. ✪ Rua 1 Dezembro 105 • Map L3 • 213 426 195 • €€€€

7 Casa do Alentejo
This Neo-Moorish former palace is home to an association for people from the Alentejo region. The restaurant is open to the public and serves simple Alentejan food in a choice of memorable rooms. ✪ Rua das Portas de Santo Antão 58 (upstairs) • Map L2 • 213 405 140 • €

8 Bonjardim Rei dos Frangos
Grilled chicken with piri-piri (chilli) is one of the fondest food memories many visitors take away from Portugal: this is one of the best purveyors. ✪ Travessa de Santo Antão 7–11 • Map L2 • 213 427 424 • €

9 Cervejaria Solmar
This classic Lisbon seafood restaurant has a wonderfully unmodernized 1950s setting. Cervejarias (beer halls) are also informal restaurants that often do seafood. ✪ Rua das Portas de Santo Antão 106 • Map L2 • 21 323 00 98 • €€€

10 Varanda de Lisboa
Great views of the Baixa can be enjoyed from the top of Hotel Mundial, whose restaurant serves a fairly classic hotel menu with a Portuguese accent. ✪ Hotel Mundial, Rua Dom Duarte 8 • Map M3 • 218 842 000 • €€€€

Left **Museu do Chiado** Right **Calçada do Duque**

Chiado & Bairro Alto

CHIADO IS WHERE SOME OF LISBON'S OLDER HILLS, *steeped in history, collided with the new cartography of Pombal's reconstructed city centre; and sparks flew, for a century at least. Today, both areas are old and venerated, and full of shops, but Chiado's history and cultural institutions give its commercial activities a gilt edge. Higher up is Bairro Alto – the "high neighbourhood" – a 16th-century maze of narrow streets framed by the wider lanes and longer blocks of later construction. It is best known as the district of Lisbon with the highest concentration of bars, but it is also a residential area and, at its western end, a quiet neighbourhood of grand old mansions.*

Praça Luís de Camões

🔟 Sights

1. Rua do Carmo and Rua Garrett
2. Largo and Convento do Carmo
3. Teatro Nacional de São Carlos
4. Museu do Chiado
5. Praça Luís de Camões
6. Elevador da Bica
7. Igreja e Museu de São Roque
8. Calçada do Duque
9. Elevador da Glória
10. Solar do Vinho do Porto

For more on the Marquis of Pombal **See p31**

1 Rua do Carmo and Rua Garrett

Chiado's main arteries flow at right angles to each other, meeting in front of Armazéns do Chiado, a shopping centre housed in the shell of a famed department store destroyed by a fire in 1988. These partially pedestrianized, mildly to steeply inclined streets are among Lisbon's most bustling, and are lined with shops old and new. Walkers up from Baixa are rewarded at the top, where the classic café A Brasileira *(see p75)* awaits. ✪ *Map L4*

2 Largo and Convento do Carmo

Accessible from Baixa using the Elevador de Santa Justa *(see p64)*, the ruin of the 14th-century Carmo church acts as a memorial to the 1755 earthquake.

Carmo church, detail of carved stone cherub

Look at the repaired rupture in one of the arches and ponder the fact that the whole structure didn't collapse. The quiet square in front of the church, littered with jacaranda blossom fallen from the trees in spring, seems an unlikely setting for one of the most dramatic events in recent Portuguese history. It was here that army tanks threatened the barracks of the National Guard, next door to the Carmo church, where Marcelo Caetano, the country's dictator, had taken refuge on 25 April 1974. His surrender ended 42 years of fascist dictatorship in Portugal. ✪ *Map L4*
• *Carmo ruin open 10am–7pm Mon–Sat (10am–6pm winter)* • *Closed Sun* • *Adm charge*

3 Teatro Nacional de São Carlos

Lisbon's opera house dates from 1793, and is regarded as the city's first Neo-Classical building. Its grand façade – the only side of the building decorated, in keeping with post-earthquake regulations – takes its cue from Milan's La Scala. But the floor plan resembles that of Naples' San Carlo opera, since destroyed in a fire. The grand interior owes more to the Baroque, with the gilt wood, marble and plush typical of opera houses. There is a café and restaurant with tables in the square *(see p75)*. ✪ *Rua Serpa Pinto 9* • *Map L5* • *21 325 30 45* • *Box office open 1–7pm Mon–Fri* • *Ticket prices vary* • *www.saocarlos.pt*

4 Museu do Chiado

One of Chiado's heavyweight cultural institutions, located in the same block as the Academy of Fine Arts, the Chiado Museum is nonetheless an unfusty place for viewing Portuguese art from the mid-19th century on. The core collection covers about 1850–1950, but recent acquisitions and temporary shows bring things up to date. ✪ *Rua Serpa Pinto 4* • *Map L5* • *Open 10am–6pm Tue–Sun* • *Adm charge* • *www.museudochiado-ipmuseus.pt*

Teatro Nacional de São Carlos

Lisbon's Liver

Bairro Alto's association with bohemian lifestyles, loose living and drinking goes back several centuries (drug-dealing is a more recent feature). Even when the area was a posh residential district in the 17th and 18th centuries – and parts of it still are – there was a shadier side. In the 19th century, newspaper offices and printing shops moved in, bringing with them a demand for cheap and somewhat unrefined entertainment. In 1833, the local authorities decided to make Bairro Alto a zone of regulated prostitution. Fado singing was closely associated with all this; today's tidied-up version is really a sort of *fado bourgeois*.

Praça Luís de Camões

This square, where Chiado meets Bairro Alto, is a favourite rendezvous. It is named after the poet laureate, whose heroic bronze, with lesser chroniclers and colleagues in stone around his feet, presides over the bright white stone oval traffic island. It used to be shaded by magnificent umbrella pines, but these have been replaced – supposedly for reasons of historical consistency – by still-puny poplars. Map K4

Elevador da Bica

Opened in 1892, this is the smallest of Lisbon's funiculars, passing through the lively neighbourhood of Bica on its way between Largo do Calhariz and Rua de São Paulo. Like Lisbon's other funiculars, it is powered by an electric motor, which moves the cable to which both cars are attached; they counterbalance each other and so lighten the motor's load. Largo do Calhariz at Rua da Bica Duarte Belo • Map K4 • Runs 7am–11pm Mon–Fri, 7am–9pm Sat & Sun • Bus/tram ticket

Igreja e Museu de São Roque

The Jesuit church of St Roch, built in the second half of the 16th century on the edge of what would become Bairro Alto, is a monument to the wealth of religious orders and to the extravagance of Dom João V – although you wouldn't know it from the outside. Inside, however, its chapel to St John the Baptist has been described as one of the most expensive ever made. It was assembled in Rome in the 1740s, from all the most precious materials available at the time, then disassembled and shipped to Lisbon to be put back together again. The church's Museum of Sacred Art, with further riches from the chapel, has an impressive collection of vestments and paintings *(see p33)*.

Calçada do Duque

This series of steps, from Largo Trindade Coelho to the bottom of Calçada do Carmo, is a treat. Along the

Elevador da Bica

Tile detail, Igreja de São Roque

gradual descent are Café Buenos Aires *(see p77)* and a number of other restaurants. The view of the Castle, foreshortened above Rossio, is perfectly framed. ❧ *Map L3*

9 **Elevador da Glória**

Lisbon's best-known and now its busiest funicular links Restauradores with Bairro Alto. The second to be built, it was inaugurated in 1885 after lengthy discussion. Formerly, the cars were open-top double-deckers, propelled by cog-rail and cable, with a water counterweight. Later on, steam power was used, but in 1915 the Glória went electric. ❧ *Praça dos Restauradores at Calçada da Glória • Map K3 • Runs 7am–midnight Mon–Thu, 7am–12:30am Fri & Sat, 8am–midnight Sun • Bus/tram ticket*

10 **Solar do Vinho do Porto**

Also known as the Port Wine Institute, this cool, lounge-like bar has existed for many years. The impressive wine list becomes rather shorter when you start to order, but be patient; some of the waiters have been in reserve longer than the older wines – and still manage to remain utterly unpassionate about port. ❧ *Rua de São Pedro de Alcântara 45 • Map K3 Open 11am–midnight Mon–Sat*

Chiado to Bairro Alto and the Bica

Morning

🕐 Begin by the **Carmo** ruin – reached, if you're coming from Baixa, via the Elevador de Santa Justa. Crossing to the bottom-left-hand corner of the square, take Travessa do Carmo, stopping for coffee at **Vertigo** *(see p75)*. Cross Largo Rafael Bordalo Pinheiro to Rua da Trindade and then Rua Nova da Trindade, on which turn right. Passing the famous **Cevejaria Trindade** on the right, you soon reach the top of **Calçada do Duque**. Straight ahead is **Igreja de São Roque**. Past the church, the street leads to the top of the **Elevador da Glória** on your left, and the **Solar do Vinho do Porto** on your right. For lunch, carry on up the street (here called Rua Dom Pedro V) and try **Charcutaria Francesa** at no.54, or **La Paparrucha** at no.18 – an Argentinian steak house with great city views.

Afternoon

After lunch, stroll and shop at your leisure in Bairro Alto, entering via **Rua da Rosa** on the other side of Rua Dom Pedro V. Meander, but keep track of Rua da Rosa, which will take you out of the area on the other side. Here, across the street, is the top of the **Elevador da Bica**. Ride it down to Rua de São Paulo and then head left towards Cais do Sodré and a drink at **O'Gilin's** or **The British Bar** *(see p68)*. Otherwise, you can walk halfway up the steep hill again and turn left into one of the narrow streets which will take you to **Miradouro de Santa Catarina** *(see p36)* and afternoon refreshments in the open air, overlooking the river.

Left **Livraria Bertrand** Centre **Luvaria Ulisses** Right **José António Tenente**

🔟 Shops

1 Luvaria Ulisses
This small gem of a shop is the only one in Portugal selling just gloves. Hand sewn, they have a lifetime guarantee for repairs. Ⓢ *Rua do Carmo 87A • Map L4*

2 Leitão & Irmão
Jewellery and silverware from a company that was appointed crown jewellers in 1875. The pieces are kept in museums and private collections the world over and at a shop in Lisbon's Ritz hotel. Ⓢ *Largo do Chiado 16 • Map L4*

3 A Carioca
Coffee beans from Africa, Asia and South America are roasted on the premises and sold either freshly ground or whole. Tea and chocolate are also available; try the chocolate from São Tomé. Ⓢ *Rua da Misericórdia 9 • Map L4*

4 José António Tenente
At the outlet store for the well-known Portuguese clothes designer José António Tenente, garments from his older collections are sold at reasonable prices. The main shop is in the Picoas Plaza shopping centre. Ⓢ *Travessa do Carmo 8 • Map L4*

5 Vista Alegre
The work of Portugal's premier porcelain maker is wide ranging: from modern to traditional designs, and from restrained tableware to exuberant decorative pieces. Ⓢ *Largo do Chiado 20–21 • Map L4*

6 Ana Salazar
Hailing from Lisbon, Ana Salazar transformed Portuguese fashion in the 1970s and is an internationally acclaimed stylist, arguably the country's best. Ⓢ *Rua do Carmo 87 • Map L4*

7 Manuel Alves & José Manuel Gonçalves
A pair of well-established designers offer chic and stylish *haute couture*, and ready-to-wear lines for men and women. Ⓢ *Rua Serpa Pinto 15B • Map L4*

8 Agência 117
One of the first alternative fashion shops in Lisbon is a place both for browsing and for hanging out. There are own-label, Jocomomola and Custo Barcelona clothes, as well as Fly London shoes. Ⓢ *Rua do Norte 117 • Map K4*

9 Armazéns do Chiado
In the carefully restored shell of what was Lisbon's poshest department store – destroyed by fire in 1988 – is the city's most central shopping centre. Larger retailers include FNAC and Sport Zone. Check out the food court for some great views. Ⓢ *Rua do Carmo 2 • Map L4*

10 Livraria Bertrand
The Bertrand chain has branches all over the city; this one is Lisbon's oldest bookshop. In its warren of rooms it stocks a wide selection of English-language titles. Ⓢ *Rua Garrett 73 • Map L4*

Left **A Brasileira** Right **Cafetaria de São Carlos**

Chiado: Cafés

A Brasileira
1 The city's most famous café is an Art Nouveau tunnel of florid stuccowork, mirrors and paintings from its 1920s heyday. The tables outside, where a bronze of poet Fernando Pessoa still lingers today, are among Lisbon's most coveted. ◉ *Rua Garrett 120 • Map L4*

Bénard
2 For many this is "the other café" next to A Brasileira. In fact, it is a tearoom with cakes and pastries superior to those of its neighbour. Its outdoor tables serve as a welcome extension to A Brasileira's often crowded terrace. ◉ *Rua Garrett 104 • Map L4*

No Chiado
3 This tranquil café is just a block from the bustle of Rua Garrett, but a world away. Al fresco tables, Internet access and light meals are all available. ◉ *Largo do Picadeiro 12 • Map L5*

Royale
4 Organic light lunches and snacks are served in this fairly new café, which has a small interior courtyard. Service is friendly. ◉ *Largo Rafael Bordalo Pinheiro 29 • Map L4*

Leitaria Académica
5 This venerable milk bar is named after Lisbon's first university. Its outdoor tables in peaceful Largo do Carmo are popular. Hearty meals are also served. ◉ *Largo do Carmo 1 • Map L4*

Sacramento
6 This place is a warren of rooms on different levels, all pleasantly cool, with whitewashed walls and bare-brick arches. The café overlooks the street; there is also a restaurant and a club. ◉ *Calçada do Sacramento 40 • Map L4*

Vertigo
7 A warm ambience permeates this café, whose heavy-framed mirrors and stained wood give it an old-style feel. Its informal service and organic snacks are, however, bang up-to-date. ◉ *Travessa do Carmo 4 • Map L4*

Cafetaria de São Carlos
8 Next to the São Carlos opera house *(see p71)* is a square that was once used as a parking lot. Now, one corner of it is a permanent terrace for the opera's restaurant and café – another peaceful Chiado perch. ◉ *Largo São Carlos 2 • Map L5*

Heróis Café Lounge
9 This airy, retro-modern café is set on two floors and has a courtyard at the back. Its clientele is mainly, but not exclusively, gay. Light meals are served. ◉ *Calçada do Sacramento 14 • Map L4*

Chá do Carmo
10 Located on a tranquil square in front of the Carmo ruins, this café offers several types of tea. The lunch menu has hot dishes, salads and home-made desserts. ◉ *Largo do Carmo 21 • Map L4*

Around Town – Chiado & Bairro Alto

Left **Portas Largas** Right **Bedroom**

Bairro Alto: Bars

1 Artis
Artis is one of Bairro Alto's most lived-in bars. It's a great place for those who like low lights, the sound of jazz, late conversation and toasted chicken sandwiches. ◈ *Rua Diário de Notícias 95 • Map K4*

2 Bedroom
At this DJ bar the aim is to break with minimalism by furnishing the interior with comfortable beds, patterned wallpaper and clever lighting. The music is hip-hop, electro and tracks from the 1980s and 1990s. ◈ *Rua do Norte 86 • Map K4*

3 Portas Largas
This is the Bairro Alto in a nutshell. "Wide Doors", as it is called, is a rustic-tavern-turned-bar, whose party spills out onto the street. It is gay, but not overwhelmingly so. ◈ *Rua Atalaia 105 • Map K3*

4 Capela
The decor of this DJ bar combines sparseness with extravagance. The deep yet narrow space can get extremely crowded – but always with an interesting mix of people. ◈ *Rua da Atalaia 45 • Map K4*

5 Catacumbas
This is a highly civilized, café-like jazz bar. There is live music occasionally; customers sometimes play the piano too. ◈ *Travessa Água da Flor 43 • Map K3*

6 Clube da Esquina
Well on the way to classic status, the "Corner Club" is a chatty, crowded, yet relaxed place whose well-lit interior with exposed wooden beams has framed many a good start to a Bairro Alto night. ◈ *Rua da Barroca 30 • Map K4*

7 Velvet
This bar has an intimate atmosphere flowing from its use of candlelight and theatrically contrasting furnishings. The music also helps: there are DJs and live acts. Wednesday is jazz night. ◈ *Rua do Norte 121 • Map K4*

8 Etílico
Comfy sofas and a varied group of resident DJs are assets of this brightly coloured DJ bar with a friendly vibe. ◈ *Rua do Grémio Lusitano 8 • Map K3*

9 Clube do Mercado
A keen, studenty crowd hangs out at this serious DJ bar with mainly black music, lots of old furniture – and free fresh fruit. Spiritually it is in Bairro Alto, even if technically it falls just outside. ◈ *Rua das Taipas 8 • Map K2*

10 Pavilhão Chinês
Among the oldest bars in Bairro Alto, this place has something completely different. Its series of rooms is decorated with collections of dolls, Airfix models, hats, coasters and the like. ◈ *Rua Dom Pedro V 89 • Map K2*

The best streets for bar-hopping are Rua da Atalaia, Rua da Barroca, Rua do Diário de Notícias and Rua do Norte.

Price Categories

For a three course	€ under €15
meal for one with half	€€ €15–€20
a bottle of wine (or	€€€ €20–€30
equivalent meal), taxes	€€€€ €30–€40
and extra charges.	€€€€€ over €40

Tavares

🔟 Restaurants

1 Tavares
Lisbon's oldest restaurant has an ornate Edwardian interior with gilded wood, stucco and red plush. The underlyingly Portuguese menu has been reignited by French chef Philippe Peudenier *(see p45)*.

2 Pap'Açorda
Açorda (see p46) is a rustic dish of the Alentejo region, here successfully modernized and glamourized. The rest of the menu also seasons tradition with a dash of innovation. It's a Lisbon classic. ॐ *Rua da Atalaia 57–9 • Map K4 • 21 346 48 11 • Closed Sun, Mon • €€€€*

3 Olivier
This dark-panelled Bairro Alto restaurant has a gourmet menu featuring choices such as sautéed foie gras with caramelized apple and balsamic sauce. ॐ *Rua do Teixeira 35 • Map K3 • 21 343 14 05 • Closed L daily; Sun • €€€€*

4 Alecrim às Flores
There are tables on the steps outside this friendly place. The mainly Portuguese dishes have a modern touch. Lamb is a good option. ॐ *Travessa do Alecrim 4 • Map K5 • 21 322 53 68 • Closed Sat L • €€€*

5 A Charcutaria
This attractive restaurant serves Portuguese fare, mainly hailing from the Alentejo region. Desserts are staunchly traditional and magnificently calorific. ॐ *Rua do Alecrim 47A • Map K5 • 21 342 38 45 • Closed Sat L; Sun • €€€€*

6 Oriente
This reliable vegetarian restaurant has an appetizing buffet spread for lunch. It caters for vegans too. ॐ *Rua Ivens 28 • Map L4 • 21 343 15 30 • €€*

7 Café Buenos Aires
On the steps between Bairro Alto and Rossio is this cosy Argentinian-inspired place with tables outside and a menu that is not all meat. ॐ *Calçada Escadinhas do Duque 31B • Map L3 • 21 342 07 39 • Closed Sun • €€*

8 Adega das Mercês
This classic Bairro Alto restaurant specializes in simple grilled fish and meat. Portions are traditionally generous – one is usually enough for two. ॐ *Travessa das Mercês 2 • Map K4 • 21 342 44 92 • Closed Sun • €€€*

9 Casanostra
One of Lisbon's first Italian restaurants remains one of its best, serving more than just good pasta. ॐ *Travessa do Poço da Cidade 60 • Map K4 • 21 342 59 31 • Closed Sat L; Mon • €€€*

10 Associação Católica Internacional ao Serviço da Juventude Feminina
A small roof-top terrace affords views of riverside Lisbon at this great lunch hideaway. It is open to the public – non-Catholics and men included. ॐ *Travessa do Ferragial 1 (top floor) • Map L5 • 21 324 09 10 • Closed D; Sat, Sun • €*

Left **Santo Amaro church** Right **Mosteiro Jerónimos, Belém**

West Lisbon

WEST LISBON COMPRISES A SERIES OF HILLS *on either side of the Alcântara valley, where a river once flowed but traffic now oozes onto the 25 de Abril bridge. The city's former aqueduct spans the valley, disappearing into the green expanse of the Monsanto Park on Lisbon's highest, broadest hill. Opposite Monsanto, the airy and desirable residential districts of Campo de Ourique, Estrela and Lapa descend in steep steps southwards towards the river. The waterfront from the Alcântara docks to Belém is a straight, accessible stretch bathed in bright light, with the 25 de Abril bridge arching overhead.*

Sights

1 Jardim Botânico
2 Casa Fernando Pessoa
3 Estrela
4 Assembleia da República
5 Museu de Arte Antiga
6 Museu da Marioneta
7 Ermida de Santo Amaro
8 Aqueduto das Águas Livres
9 Monsanto
10 Belém

Jardim Botânico

Preceding pages **The huge pavement compass in front of the Padrão dos Descobrimentos (Monument to the Discoveries)**

1 Jardim Botânico

Central Lisbon's sloping botanic garden was laid out in the second half of the 19th century, becoming the main showcase for exotic flora – taking over from Ajuda's botanic garden due to its more central location. Buildings at the top of the garden now house various museums, including an ageing but child-friendly Science Museum *(see p51)*. ✎ *Rua da Escola Politécnica • Map J1–2 • 21 392 18 30 • Garden open 9am (10am Sat, Sun)–8pm (6pm in winter) • Adm charge*

2 Casa Fernando Pessoa

Portugal's great modernist poet Fernando Pessoa lived in this building from 1920 until his death in 1935. Later acquired and comprehensively redesigned by the city council, in 1993 it opened as a museum dedicated to Pessoa and to poetry. It houses the poet's personal library, books about him, and a collection of Portuguese and foreign poetry. There is also a space for temporary exhibitions and events, some of Pessoa's furniture, and the poet's room, which was left unaltered and is "recreated" at irregular intervals by invited artists. A pleasant restaurant is set in the small modernist-style back garden. ✎ *Rua Coelho da Rocha 16–18 • Map E4 • 21 391 32 70 • Open 10am–6pm Mon–Wed, Fri; 1–8pm Thu • Adm free*

Music pavilion, Jardim da Estrela

3 Estrela

The area between Campo de Ourique and Lapa takes its name from the Estrela basilica *(see p32)*, opposite the entrance to central Lisbon's most agreeable park, Jardim da Estrela. It is also a distinctly British part of Lisbon, with the British embassy, cemetery (where Henry Fielding lies) and hospital (now British in name only). ✎ *Praça da Estrela • Map E4*

4 Assembleia da República

This building has been the seat of the Portuguese parliament since 1833, when the Benedictine monks of the Convento de São Bento da Saúde were evicted – a year before the official dissolution of religious orders. The vast monastery was adapted in fits and starts; today's formal Neo-Classical building was designed at the end of the 19th century. In a city of hills and impressive prospects, it sits surprisingly humbly at the bottom of a hill. ✎ *Largo das Cortes • Map F4 • 21 391 96 25 • Visits by appointment only • Free*

Assembleia da República

A Golden Gate for Europe

By the time the steel suspension bridge was built across the Tejo in 1962–6, bridges had been proposed at various sites for nearly a century. Similar in design to San Francisco's Golden Gate bridge, Ponte Salazar (as it was originally called, after Portugal's dictator) is just over 1km (over half a mile) long, making it Europe's longest bridge in 1966. Its two towers are just under 200m (650ft) tall. Renamed Ponte 25 de Abril after the Carnation Revolution of that date in 1974, it has been adapted to increasing traffic over the 40 years of its existence by squeezing in extra lanes and adding a railway crossing underneath the roadway. By the early 1990s, however, its traffic jams were getting notorious. The 1998 opening of the Vasco da Gama bridge (also briefly the longest in Europe) has taken some of the pressure off.

5 Museu de Arte Antiga

Portugal's national museum holds some of the country's greatest artistic treasures, as well as foreign masterpieces such as Bosch's *The Temptations of St Anthony* – not in fact St Anthony of Padua, one of Lisbon's patron saints, but the Egyptian St Anthony, founder of Christian monasticism *(see pp14–15)*.

6 Museu da Marioneta

Lisbon's Puppet Museum has a collection of over 800 puppets from all over the world, as well as scenery, props and machinery for puppet shows. It is housed in a former convent which it shares with housing and the gourmet restaurant A Travessa *(see p44)*. The museum also holds shows and puppet-making workshops for school groups. ✎ *Rua da Esperança 146 (Convento das Bernardas)* • *Map F5* • *21 394 28 10* • *Open 10am–12:30pm, 2–5:30pm Tue–Sun* • *Adm charge*

7 Ermida de Santo Amaro

The architectural and artistic appeal of this small hilltop chapel is much greater than its rather few tourist visitors would suggest. And there's a good view. It was built in the mid-16th century to an unusual, seven-sided plan, survived the 1755 earthquake and is decorated with 16th-, 17th- and 18th-century tile panels. They show the miracles of Santo Amaro, patron saint of those who suffer fractured limbs, as well as the legend about the original chapel's founders: Galician seamen who had been shipwrecked at the mouth of the Tejo. ✎ *Calçada de Santo Amaro* • *Map C5* • *Knock on door or ask nearby if closed* • *Free*

8 Aqueduto das Águas Livres

Lisbon's long-legged aqueduct was built just over a decade before the 1755 earthquake – which it survived, continuing to supply water to the shattered city. Some facts and figures: the 35 arches marching across the Alcântara valley are up to 64 m

Museu da Marioneta

Note that young children may find some of the puppets at the Museu da Marioneta frightening.

Aqueduto das Águas Livres

(210 ft) high, making them the tallest stone arches in the world at the time they were built; the aqueduct's span is nearly 1 km (half a mile); the main water source was 58 km (36 miles) of ducting away; the system was only taken out of service in 1967. The Museu da Água organizes walks across the aqueduct.
Ⓢ *Map E2–D2* • *21 810 02 15*

9 Monsanto

Monsanto is the big green bit on the maps; Lisbon's largest wooded area and its highest hill. Encroached on by construction, bisected by a motorway and blighted by prostitution and other criminality, this is still the best place to go near central Lisbon for the smell of pine trees, a fresh breeze and a walk with soil underfoot. There are a number of fenced-off recreational areas, including children's parks *(see p50)*, tennis courts, a shooting range, a campsite and a rugby pitch. It's an area well worth exploring – in daylight. Ⓢ *Map D2*

10 Belém

Now part of a larger city, rather than the distant suburb it was in the pre-motorized era, Lisbon's westernmost district nonetheless retains pleasant contrasts with the city centre. Refreshing river breezes and a cluster of some of Lisbon's main sights contribute to its appeal *(see pp84–5).*

A Walk through West Lisbon

Morning

🕐 Begin by catching the 28 tram to its terminus at **Prazeres**. Visit the cemetery of the same name, if cemeteries are of interest, then stroll along Rua Saraiva de Carvalho past the large **Santo Condestável** church (with its attractive stained-glass windows). Drop into **Campo de Ourique** market *(see p40)* and pick up some fresh fruit, or just whet your appetite for lunch. Then head right along Rua Coelho da Rocha and visit **Casa Fernando Pessoa**. Lunch here, or at the small Italian deli called **Maria da Fonte**, in Rua Quatro de Infantaria.

Afternoon

After lunch, walk all the way down Rua Coelho da Rocha, turn right into Rua da Estrela, and proceed downhill to one of the corner entrances of **Jardim da Estrela**, where you can absorb the mid-city peace of the park. When you're ready, head for the main entrance of the park and you'll see the **Basílica de Estrela** across the square. After a visit, make your way slowly through Lapa via Rua João de Deus, which enters it on the left of the basilica. Follow the tram tracks round and then down Rua de São Domingos – veer off to left or right for extended Lapa views. Return to Rua de São Domingos and continue down it until you reach steps (there's a tile-making factory here, with a shop), which will take you down to Rua das Janelas Verdes and the **Museu de Arte Antiga** *(see pp14–15).*

Check out http://museudaagua.epal.pt for more information on walks across the aqueduct.

Left **Museu da Marinha (front façade)** Right **Padrão dos Descobrimentos (eastern face)**

TOP10 Belém: Sights

1 Mosteiro dos Jerónimos
Portugal's greatest national monument is emblematic of the country's Manueline style. Dom Manuel I built the monastery and abbey in the early 16th century, in thanks for Portugal's voyages of maritime discovery *(see pp10–11)*.

2 Museu de Arqueologia
Housed in the west wing of the Mosteiro dos Jerónimos, this museum exhibits Portuguese archeological finds from the Iron Age onwards. ✎ *Praça do Império • Map A6 • 21 362 00 00 • Open 10am–6pm Tue–Sun • Adm charge*

3 Museu da Marinha
The naval museum in the west wing of the Mosteiro dos Jerónimos covers shipbuilding and navigation. ✎ *Praça do Império • Map A6 • 21 362 00 19 • Open 10am–5pm (6pm in summer) Tue–Sun • Adm charge*

4 Torre de Belém
For many, this perfectly proportioned defensive tower is the masterpiece of the Manueline style. When built in 1515–20, it was almost mid-stream in the Tejo; land on the right bank was later reclaimed *(see pp18–19)*.

5 Palácio de Belém
This 16th-century palace, much altered by Dom João V in the 18th century, is the working residence of Portugal's president. ✎ *Praça Afonso de Albuquerque • Map A6 • 21 361 46 00 • Open 10am–6pm Sat (guided visit) • Adm charge*

6 Museu dos Coches
Lisbon's popular museum of historic coaches is housed in the former riding school of the Palácio de Belém *(see p34)*.

7 Centro Cultural de Belém
Constructed for use during Portugal's 1992 EU presidency, the CCB is home to cultural events from music, to film and theatre *(see p34)*.

8 Padrão dos Descobrimentos
Created in 1960 for the 500th anniversary of the death of Henry the Navigator, this monument is in the form of the prow of a ship. There is a multimedia show called the Lisbon Experience housed here. ✎ *Avenida de Brasília • Map B6 • 21 303 19 50 • Open 9am–5pm (7pm in summer) Mon–Sun • Adm charge for lift*

9 Jardim Museu Agrícola Tropical
This garden of tropical trees and plants – the research centre of the Institute for Tropical Sciences – is an oasis in the tourist bustle of Belém. ✎ *Largo dos Jerónimos • Map B5–6 • 21 363 70 23 • Open 9am–6pm daily; 9am–5pm Mon–Fri, 11am–5pm Sat & Sun (winter) • Adm charge*

10 Palácio da Ajuda
The Neo-Classical palace in Ajuda was left unfinished in 1807 when the royal family was forced into exile in Brazil. ✎ *Calçada da Ajuda • Map B5 • 21 363 70 95 • Open 10am–5pm Thu–Tue • Adm charge*

Price Categories

For a three course
meal for one with half
a bottle of wine (or
equivalent meal), taxes
and extra charges.

€ under €15
€€ €15–€20
€€€ €20–€30
€€€€ €30–€40
€€€€€ over €40

Ton Xin

TOP10 Belém: Restaurants

1 Belém Bar Café
This large bar, restaurant and nightclub affords views through a glass wall to the riverside. The Mediterranean-style food pleases a fairly sharp crowd. ⊗ *Avenida de Brasília, Pavilhão Poente • Map C6 • 21 362 42 32 • Closed Mon & Sat L; Sun • €€€€*

2 Já Sei
This Belém classic produces Portuguese and international cuisine with a certain formal flair. ⊗ *Avenida de Brasília 202 • Map A6 • 21 301 59 69 • Closed Sun D; Mon • €€€€*

3 Vela Latina
Overlooking the Doca do Bom Sucesso near the Torre de Belém, this pleasant restaurant with a terrace specializes in creatively prepared fish and seafood. Meat dishes include quail in raspberry sauce. ⊗ *Doca do Bom Sucesso • Map A6 • 21 301 71 18 • Closed Sun • €€€€*

4 Ton Xin
Occupying most of the main pavilion over the pool near the Padrão dos Descobrimentos, one of Lisbon's largest Chinese restaurants offers good value. ⊗ *Avenida de Brasília, Edifício Espelho de Água • Map A6 • 21 301 66 52 • €€*

5 Belém Terrace
A large roof terrace is the great attraction of this restaurant and bar by Belém's marina. The food is unfussy pasta, steaks and salads. ⊗ *Avenida de Brasília, Doca de Belém • Map B6 • 21 362 08 65 • €€*

6 Cais de Belém
Next to the Jardim de Belém, the traditional Cais de Belém does a reliable *arroz de peixe com gambas* (fish rice with prawns). ⊗ *Rua Vieira Portuense 64 • Map B6 • 21 362 15 37 • Closed Tue D; Wed • €€€*

7 Picanha de Belém
This lively place specializes in flavourful *picanha*, a Brazilian cut of rump steak, grilled and served with stewed black beans, rice, baked potatoes and salad. For non-carnivores there's grilled fillet of grouper. ⊗ *Rua Vieira Portuense 78 • Map B6 • 21 365 83 00 • €€€*

8 Estufa Real
Set in former greenhouses in Ajuda's botanical garden, this restaurant serves Portuguese fare. Sunday brunch is popular. ⊗ *Calçada do Galvão (Jardim Botânico da Ajuda) • Map B5 • 21 361 94 00 • Closed D; Sat • €€€*

9 In Rio Lounge
With a popular terrace, a retro-groovy bar and a slightly more formal restaurant, this low building on the riverside is busy all day. Grilled fish and seafood dominate the menu. ⊗ *Avenida de Brasília, Pavilhão Nascente 311 • Map C6 • 21 362 62 48 • €€€*

10 Os Jerónimos
This simple bar-restaurant provides a serious take on traditional Portuguese food. Portions are large. ⊗ *Rua de Belém 74 • Map B6 • 21 363 84 23 • Closed Sat • €€€*

Left **West Lisbon waterfront, with Ponte 25 de Abril and Cristo Rei** Right **Jardim Botânico da Ajuda**

🔟 West Lisbon: Best of the Rest

1 Antiga Confeitaria de Belém
This celebrated café and pastry shop is the originator of *pastéis de Belém* – custard tarts known as *pastéis de nata* elsewhere. ⊗ Rua de Belém 84–92 • Map B6

2 Coisas do Arco do Vinho
Within the CCB, one of the best wine shops in Lisbon excels with its quality Portuguese wines from smaller producers. ⊗ Rua Bartolomeu Dias, units 7–8 • Map A6

3 The Berardo Collection
One of the world's largest collections of modern art *(see p27)* has recently moved into the Centro Cultural de Belém. Ironically enough, Madeiran tycoon Joe Berardo accumulated his collection with the help of Francisco Capelo, creator of the design museum now displaced by the Berardo Collection *(see p34)*.

4 Fundação Museu Arpad Szenes-Vieira da Silva
Housed in a former silk factory, this museum is dedicated to the work of Portuguese Modernist painter Maria Helena Vieira da Silva and her Hungarian husband, Arpad Szenes *(see p35)*.

5 Waterfront to Belém
A family favourite for Sunday strolling and biking, the riverside promenade runs almost uninterrupted from the Docas area to the Torre de Belém *(see pp18–19)*. ⊗ Avenida de Brasília • Map C6

6 Jardim Botânico da Ajuda
Portugal's oldest botanical garden, was laid out in 1768. It has a vast 400-year-old Madeiran dragon tree and box hedges. The Estufa Real *(see p85)* serves lunch. ⊗ Calçada da Ajuda • Map B5 • 21 362 25 03 • Open daily 9am–6pm (8pm in summer); closed Wed • Free

7 Lapa streets
Stroll past Lapa's many grand residences and humbler homes for an essential Lisbon contrast, and exhilarating topography. ⊗ Rua de São Caetano, Rua do Sacramento, Rua de São Félix • Map E4–5

8 Docas area
Overlooking the Santo Amaro marina, this waterfront row of converted warehouses is one of Lisbon's most buzzing bar, restaurant and nightlife areas. ⊗ Doca de Santo Amaro • Map D5

9 Miradouro de Santa Catarina
This central Lisbon viewing point overlooking the river is a popular place to meet for a beer or a coffee. Thankfully, few visitors seem much awed by the hirsute and hollow-eyed statue of Adamastor *(see p36)*.

10 Igreja da Memória
This Neo-Classical church was built in 1760 to give thanks for the narrow escape Dom José I had from an assassination attempt. ⊗ Calçada do Galvão • Map B5 • Open 4–6pm Mon–Sat • Free

 Share your travel recommendations on traveldk.com

Águia no Bico

Price Categories

For a three course meal for one with half a bottle of wine (or equivalent meal), taxes and extra charges.

€ under €15
€€ €15–€20
€€€ €20–€30
€€€€ €30–€40
€€€€€ over €40

10 Gay Lisbon

1 Frágil
Popular club owned by musician and composer Rodrigo Leão, with an underlying theme that stretches back to the 1980s. The crowd is a mix of gay men, lesbians and a scattering of heterosexuals. ◎ *Rua da Atalaia 126 • Map K4*

2 Sertório Sauna Club
One of Lisbon's newer saunas offers facilities that include Jacuzzis, a Turkish bath, saunas and a bar. ◎ *Calçada da Patriarcal 34 • Map F4*

3 Restaurante Memories das Tias
This small restaurant has an almost exclusively gay and lesbian clientele. It serves ambitiously prepared food in a friendly, intimate atmosphere. ◎ *Travessa da Palmeira 46 • Map F4 • 21 346 48 87 • Closed L; Mon • €€€*

4 Trumps
A classic of Lisbon's gay scene, this mixed club has several bar areas, a dance floor and a snooker room, spread over two levels. ◎ *Rua da Imprensa Nacional 104B • Map F4*

5 Água no Bico
This gay bar attracts a crowd that is mixed in terms of age. Those wishing to surf the web can take advantage of Internet access. You'll need to ring the doorbell to get in. ◎ *Rua de São Marçal 170 • Map F4*

6 Finalmente
Another fixture of the Lisbon gay scene, Finalmente has a tiny dance floor and notorious drag shows. It gets going late – but when it does, it really does. ◎ *Rua da Palmeira 38 • Map F4*

7 Bric-a-Bar
This long-established and fairly spacious gay bar is a cruising spot. There is a choice of bars as well as a dance floor. ◎ *Rua Cecílio de Sousa 82–4 • Map F4*

8 Memorial
Although nominally a lesbian club, this place has a fairly mixed clientele. Entertainment comes in the form of regular transvestite and comedy shows. There is a small dance floor. ◎ *Rua Gustavo Matos Sequeira 42A • Map F4*

9 Max
Attracting a slightly older clientele, this gay bar has occasional strip shows and message nights – when you can leave a message for someone who caught your fancy and see if it is reciprocated. ◎ *Rua de São Marçal 15 • Map F4*

10 SS Bar
This relaxed mixed bar has a friendly atmosphere and doesn't feel like a cruising joint. Like most gay bars, it's a late starter. There are transvestite shows on Fridays and Saturdays. Ring the doorbell to enter. ◎ *Calçada da Patriarcal 38 • Map F4*

Left **Eclectic decor at Paródia** Right **Incógnito**

Top 10 Nightlife

Estado Líquido
One of the seminal clubs in the Santos area has a relaxed DJ vibe and live music at weekends. A hip sushi bar opens till late upstairs. ⊗ *Largo de Santos 5A • Map F4*

Foxtrot
With a rambling series of rooms, a courtyard, pool tables and kitschy decor, this old-style bar has become a quintessential Lisbon milieu. ⊗ *Travessa de Santa Teresa 28 • Map F4*

Incógnito
The name and door bell might suggest otherwise, but this is one of Lisbon's best venues for dancing the night away. The 80s nostalgia has been a constant; now it's mixed with newer sounds (see p42).

Paradise Garage
Check out this ex-warehouse venue for live music, often from outside the mainstream, by local and international bands. The weekend after-hours sessions, with softer DJ sounds, are legendary (see p42).

Indochina
Indochina is one of a quartet of purpose-converted warehouse clubs in the riverfront area between Santos and Alcântara. It is retro-modern in style, with a bar and restaurant, and has a calmer atmosphere than some of its competitors. ⊗ *Rua da Cintura do Porto de Lisboa, Armazém F • Map D5*

Kremlin
This classic Lisbon dance-music venue is still throbbing to the sound of house. Nearby Kapital and Konvento have the same owners, if somewhat different crowds – but at dawn all converge on Kremlin, arriving through internal passageways (see p42).

Speakeasy
This easy-going live music venue and somewhat overpriced restaurant is found down at the docks. Jazz, blues and funk are its specialities, with Monday night jam sessions. ⊗ *Cais das Oficinas, Armazém 115 • Map D5*

Nova Alcântara
The current heir to Lisbon's legendary Alcântara-Mar club is living up to most of the high expectations placed on it. Expect serious dancing, drinking and flaunting (see p42).

Paródia
Dating from the mid-1970s, this miniature bar has retained the decor of that era. If you remember the 70s, the effect is nostalgic; if you don't, it's intriguing. Ring the bell. ⊗ *Rua do Patrocínio 26B • Map E4*

Buddha Lx
Housed in the attractive Modernist Alcântara port terminal, Buddha Lx offers deep-house dancing, drinking and chill-out lounging in an oriental-inspired setting (see p42).

Also on the riverfront between Alcântara and Santos, check out Blues, Dock's Club and Queen's.

Price Categories

For a three course meal for one with half a bottle of wine (or equivalent meal), taxes and extra charges.	€ under €15
	€€ €15–€20
	€€€ €20–€30
	€€€€ €30–€40
	€€€€€ over €40

Waiters prepare for an evening at Kais

🏆10 Restaurants

Alcântara Café

When this stunning bar and pleasantly cosmopolitan restaurant opened in the late 1980s, Lisbon had neither seen nor tasted its like. It still impresses. ◈ *Rua Maria Luísa Holstein 15 • Map D5 • 21 363 71 76 • Closed L daily • €€€€*

Tromba Rija

An offshoot of a famous restaurant in Leiria, this riverside place serves Portuguese fare. ◈ *Rua do Cintura do Porto de Lisboa, Edifício 254, Armazém I • Map E5 • 21 397 15 07 • Closed Sun D; Mon L • €€€€*

Aya Bistrôt

The Aya restaurants are often regarded as serving the city's best Japanese food. At this one, it arrives on a conveyor belt. ◈ *Galerias Twin Towers, Rua de Campolide 351 • Map E2 • 21 727 11 55 • €€*

Kais/Adega do Kais

Housed in an awe-inspiring former engine shed, Kais offers a lightly modernized Portuguese menu. In the basement, the Adega do Kais is a traditional *rodízio*; customers are served from a selection of 20 dishes, for a fixed price. ◈ *Rua do Cintura do Porto de Lisboa, Cais da Viscondessa • Map E5 • 21 393 29 31 • Closed L; Sun • €€€*

Terra

This lovely vegetarian restaurant serves vegetable and meat-substitute dishes, as well as sushi. ◈ *Rua da Palmeira 15 • Map E4 • 70 710 81 08 • €€*

Nariz de Vinho Tinto

This tasting restaurant has an ambitious menu of traditional Portuguese dishes. The customer is offered a select range of everything, from mineral waters to olive oils and coffees – not to mention the actual menu and wine list. ◈ *Rua do Conde 75 • Map E5 • 21 395 30 35 • Closed Sat & Sun L & Mon • €€€€*

Clube de Jornalistas

Housed in the building of a Portuguese journalists' club, this attractive restaurant has an inner courtyard and serves top-notch modern international food. ◈ *Rua das Trinas 129 • Map E4 • 21 397 71 38 • Closed Sun • €€€*

Tasquinha d'Adelaide

A long-time neighbourhood favourite, Adelaide specializes in the cuisine of northern Portugal. The space is small and intimate. ◈ *Rua do Patrocínio 70–74 • Map E4 • 21 396 22 39 • Closed Sun • €€€*

O Mercado

What better place for a restaurant than in the same building as a food market? O Mercado cooks local food with verve. ◈ *Mercado Rosa Agulhas, Rua Leão de Oliveira • Map D5 • 21 364 91 13 • Closed Sun • €€*

A Travessa

Set in a convent building, this is one of Lisbon's most characterful restaurants in terms both of location and food *(see p44)*.

Around Town – West Lisbon

Left **Theatre Museum, Parque do Monteiro-Mor** Right **Dolphins performing at Jardim Zoológico**

Avenida & North Lisbon

AVENIDA DA LIBERDADE EXTENDS NORTHWARDS *from Restauradores for just over a kilometre (more than half a mile), at a slight incline. It ends at the roundabout named after the Marquis of Pombal, who became Lisbon's strong man after the 1755 earthquake. He stands at the centre of the swirl of traffic, flanked by a lion, surveying the city centre he created. If you carry on up to the top of Eduardo VII park and look to your right, Lisbon's early 20th-century northern extensions (now very much a part of the "centre") stretch out before you. Closer at hand is the esteemed Gulbenkian museum; further afield, the 21st-century vistas of Parque das Nações.*

🔟 Sights

1. Rotunda Marquês de Pombal/Parque Eduardo VII
2. Museu Gulbenkian
3. Avenidas Novas
4. Campo Pequeno
5. Museu da Cidade
6. Football Stadiums
7. Parque do Monteiro-Mor
8. Palácio dos Marqueses da Fronteira
9. Jardim Zoológico
10. Parque das Nações

Nymph fountain, Parque Eduardo VII

Odivelas • IC17 • IC16 • IP1 · A2 • Portela Airport • Encarnação • Lumiar • 7 • Pontinha • IC19 • 6 Campo Grande • IP1 · A1 • Olivais • Estação do Oriente • Colégio Militar / Luz • 6 • 5 • Campo Grande • Chelas • 10 • Benfica • 9 Jardim Zoológico • 4 • Parque Florestal de Monsanto • 8 • 2 Campo Pequeno • Entrecampos • Estação Braço de Prata • IP1 · A2 • São Sebastião • 3 Saldanha • Xabregas • IC15 · A5 • N117 • Campolide • Estefânia • 1 Marquês de Pombal • Graça • Tejo • miles 0 km • 2 • 4

Around Town – Avenida & North Lisbon

Sign up for DK's email newsletter on traveldk.com

1 Rotunda Marquês de Pombal/Parque Eduardo VII

The roundabout where Pombal and his lion pose was the northern limit of the city he conceived. The orderly park behind him was first laid out in the late 19th century, as a green extension of Avenida da Liberdade – and to replace the pedestrian Passeio Público that the Avenida had usurped. In 1903, Parque da Liberdade was renamed in honour of the visiting English King Edward VII. It is really more of a promenade – and its incline makes it a demanding one – than a park. For proper greenery, seek out the Estufa Fria and Estufa Quente greenhouses along the northwestern edge of the park. A walk to the top is rewarded with good views of central Lisbon. At the very top are the pleasant Linha d'Água café and Eleven restaurant (see p44). ◎ Map F2–3

Neo-Moorish façade, Campo Pequeno

Avenida da República, and 21st-century shopping has come to Praça Duque de Saldanha, but this area of Lisbon is still a respectable residential one. ◎ Map F1–2

2 Museu Gulbenkian

The museum founded on the collections and fortune of Armenian exile Calouste Gulbenkian is one of Lisbon's most satisfying tourist sights (see pp24–5).

3 Avenidas Novas

The "New Avenues" – now a century old – are an uneven grid of streets immediately to the north of Pombal and Parque Eduardo VII. The area is a fairly typical example of late 19th- to early 20th-century planning: wide streets have tree-lined lanes down the middle, and grand residences line the main avenues. It became the heart of a newer, upper-middle-class Lisbon, away from the crowded conditions and perceived insalubriousness of the old riverside districts. It has been much altered along its main axis,

Lalique at Museu Gulbenkian

4 Campo Pequeno

One of Lisbon's most striking buildings, the Campo Pequeno bullring is a delightful arabic-oriental pastiche from 1892 with onion cupolas and keyhole windows. It stands on a spot where bullfights (see p92) have been held since at least the first half of the 18th century. The area was then part of a vast terrain of country estates a short ride from the centre. It reopened in 2006 after several years of repair and underground extension which created a modern leisure and shopping complex lit by discrete light wells. None of this is meant to intrude on the drama played out in the ring, which can also be roofed over for use as a concert or show venue. ◎ Map F1
• 21 782 05 75 • Bullfights traditionally on Thu, May–Sep • Adm for events varies

5 Museu da Cidade

The city museum is housed in an 18th-century palace, Palácio Pimenta, at the top of Campo Grande. The palace itself is worth seeing, in particular for the kitchen's "still-life" tiles depicting animal carcasses hung to tenderize. The permanent exhibition traces Lisbon's development from the earliest settlements on the banks of the Tejo. Perhaps the most evocative display is the large three-dimensional model of Lisbon as it is believed to have looked before the earthquake in 1755. ◉ Campo Grande 245 • Map C1 • 21 751 3200 • Open 10am–1pm, 2–6pm Tue–Sun • Adm charge

Tiled terrace leading to the chapel of the Palácio Fronteira

Riding Against the Bull

Portuguese bullfighting is always introduced with the qualification that the bull isn't killed. This attempt to appease opponents of bullfighting (and possibly the bulls themselves) is both misguided and disingenuous. In fact the bull is unceremoniously slaughtered after the fight – surely a rather academic distinction from the animal's perspective. The most interesting difference compared with Spanish bullfighting – once you recognize that both forms successively wound the animal in order to make the finale possible – is that a rider on an unprotected horse (the bull's horns are wrapped) performs an equestrian ballet with the bull, while sticking short spears in between its shoulder blades to make its head hang lower. The finale is then performed by a group of intrepid forcados on foot, who charge the bull in single file, throwing themselves between its horns and over one side in order to topple it and hold it fast.

6 Football Stadiums

Lisbon's two major football teams, Benfica and Sporting, both built new stadiums – on the sites of their respective old ones – for the Euro 2004 championship, held in Portugal. Sporting's Estádio José Alvalade is a green and yellow cake tin (team colours are actually green and white) on the northern city limits, not far from the airport. A short distance west along the Segunda Circular ring road, opposite the enormous Colombo shopping centre, sits Benfica's Estádio da Luz, an airier edifice reminiscent of a helix on its side; it's partly painted red, the team colour. Both stadiums also incorporate modern leisure complexes. ◉ Rua Fernando da Fonseca; Avenida General Norton de Matos • Map B1 • 21 751 6000; 21 721 9500 • Match tickets around €10

7 Parque do Monteiro-Mor

Despite its unpromising location next to one of the major northern exits from Lisbon, this lovely Italianate park is one of the city's best oases. With its palace – now housing two moderately interesting museums those of Theatre and Costume – it is a reminder of what Lisbon's hinterland was once like. ◉ Largo Júlio de Castilho • Map B1 • 21 759 0318 • Open 10am–6pm Tue–Sun • Adm charge (covers park and both museums)

8 Palácio dos Marqueses da Fronteira

A 17th-century former hunting pavilion, expanded after the 1755 earthquake, this manor house and its gardens are one of Lisbon's most rewarding sights. The formal gardens are full of statues and tiled panels, from busts of Portuguese kings to allegorical representations of the seasons and the zodiac. Highlights inside the palace include the Battle Room, with depictions of battles during the War of Restoration against Spain – in which the first Marquis fought. Fronteira Palace is still owned and lived in by the 12th Marquis, who collects contemporary art and sometimes stages exhibitions. ✆ *Largo de São Domingos de Benfica 1 • Map B2 • 21 778 2023 • Guided tours Mon–Sat (Jun–Sep: 10:30am, 11am, 11:30am, noon; Oct–May: 11am, noon) • Adm charge*

9 Jardim Zoológico

Lisbon's Zoo is a sprightly centenarian, incorporating a small amusement park as well as the usual incarcerated beasts *(see p50)*.

10 Parque das Nações

The former Expo 98 site is now a business and leisure area, with exhibition spaces, events venues and a variety of sights *(see pp16–17)*.

Knowledge Pavilion, Parque das Nações

To the Gulbenkian and Beyond

Morning

Begin at the **Pombal roundabout**. An underpass leads to the statue, where you can study its various representations of tidal waves and destruction, as well as of the enlightened despot's many reforms. Cross back to the bottom of **Parque Eduardo VII** and set out for the summit; in summertime it's best not to leave it too late in the morning, as the walk is unshaded and it gets hot early. If you need a break, dive into the cool of the **Estufa Fria** and **Quente greenhouses**. At the top, ponder the symbolism of João Cutileiro's *Monument to 25 April* – not one of his most communicative works – and its contrast with Keil do Amaral's **twin columns**. Then climb the last bit of the hill to **Linha d'Água**; lunch here, or at the adjacent **Eleven**, whose Michelin star is deserved.

Afternoon

After lunch, continue past **El Corte Inglés** and on to the side entrance of the **Gulbenkian Museum**, at the north end of Avenida António Augusto de Aguiar. Expect to spend most of the afternoon in the museum – or else give it a quick browse and decide what to come back for. Stroll through the park and exit it on Rua Marquês de Sá Bandeira, then take Avenida Miguel Bombarda for a taste of the **Avenidas Novas**. Turn left on to Avda da República and walk a few blocks north to **Campo Pequeno** and its Neo-Moorish bullring. Even if you disapprove of bull-fighting you can enjoy a drink in the park surrounding the whimsical arena.

Left **Jazz at Hot Clube** Right **Centro Colombo shopping centre**

TOP10 Best of the Rest

1 Hot Clube
Lisbon's oldest jazz club seems always to have been here, indifferent to shifting fashions. It is the kind of small basement club where the gap between artists and audience evaporates. ◈ *Praça da Alegria 38 • Map K1*

2 Avenida Designer Shops
The former Passeio Público (Public Promenade) still hasn't recovered from the introduction of vehicles over a century ago. However, the appearance of international designer shops attests that Lisbon's main avenue has regained some of its pedigree. ◈ *Avenida da Liberdade • Map F3*

3 El Corte Inglés
The Spanish chain has one of its largest complexes in Lisbon, including the city's only true department store – plus restaurants, cinemas and luxury apartments. ◈ *Avenida António Augusto de Aguiar • Map F2*

4 Parque da Bela Vista
A large urban park, Bela Vista hosts the Rock in Rio festival, which takes place every 2 years (next one will be in 2010). ◈ *Avenida Gago Coutinho*

5 Maxime
Formerly a grand cabaret venue, then a strip joint, Maxime has recently reinvented itself as a stage for a rich variety of musical performances. ◈ *Praça da Alegria 58 • Map K1*

6 Culturgest
Housed in the vast postmodern headquarters of a state-owned bank, Culturgest stages music, dance, theatre and exhibitions *(see p35)*.

7 Benfica
This northwestern suburb of Lisbon, now very much a part of the city, has its own rhythm. The famous football team did not start up here – it moved in – but this is still one of Lisbon's proudest *bairros*. ◈ *Estrada de Benfica • Map B2*

8 Alameda
In a part of the city where tourists rarely venture, Alameda's narrow common and its Mussolini-esque lighted fountain provide a sense of Lisbon as it was before 1974. ◈ *Alameda Dom Afonso Henriques, Avenida Almirante Reis • Map G1*

9 Centro Colombo
Described as the biggest shopping centre in the Iberian peninsula, Colombo has a staggering 420 shops, 60 restaurants and 10 cinemas. ◈ *Avenida Lusíada • Map B2 • 10am–midnight daily*

10 Museu Rafael Bordalo Pinheiro
This museum dedicated to Portugal's best-known caricaturist political lampoonist and ceramic artist offers a thorough but light-hearted look at Portugal's history and temperament. ◈ *Campo Grande 382 • Map C1 • 21 755 04 68 • Open 10am–6pm Tue–Sun • Adm charge*

Around Town – Avenida and North Lisbon

Other jazz venues include Netjazzcafé at Chapitô, and Ondajazz Bar (see p60)

Price Categories

For a three course meal for one with half a bottle of wine (or equivalent meal), taxes and extra charges.	€ under €15
	€€ €15–€20
	€€€ €20–€30
	€€€€ €30–€40
	€€€€€ over €40

Enoteca

Restaurants and Cafés

1 Luca
Integrating Italian cuisine with Iberian ingredients, Luca is much more than just another pasta place. The space, an old chrome-plating workshop, is bright and modern. ◈ *Rua de Santa Marta 35 • Map F3 • 21 315 02 12 • Closed Sat L; Sun • €€€*

2 Eleven
Lisbon's premier gourmet restaurant is a recent addition at the top of Parque Eduardo VII *(see p37)*. Its modern Mediterranean food by Joachim Koerper has earned the city its only current Michelin star *(see p44)*.

3 Ribadouro
This is one of the city's best *cervejarias* (beer halls). Like many, it specializes in seafood, some of it pricey. ◈ *Avda da Liberdade 155 • Map K1 • 21 354 94 11 • €€*

4 Enoteca
The city's most appealing wine bar serves tasty small dishes to go with its wide choice of wines. ◈ *Rua da Mãe d'Água • Map J2 • 21 342 20 79 • Closed L; Mon • €€€*

5 Psi
This vegetarian restaurant offers dishes from around the world in a garden setting – and a spiritual vibe. The Dalai Lama dropped by on a visit to Lisbon. ◈ *Alameda Santo António dos Capuchos, Jardim dos Sabores • Map G3 • 21 359 05 73 • Closed Sun • €*

6 Assuka
One of Lisbon's best-value Japanese restaurants offers great sushi and friendly service. ◈ *Rua de São Sebastião 150 • Map F2 • 21 314 93 45 • Closed Sun L • €€*

7 Café Mexicana
This busy café and restaurant in the Guerra Junqueiro/Roma shopping area provides a neat slice of middle-class Lisbon life, along with coffee and ample pastries. The 1960s interior has a certain something. ◈ *Avenida Guerra Junqueiro 30 • Map G1*

8 Magnolia Caffé
Lisbon has several branches of this modern, ambitious café chain. This, like the others, combines tasteful surroundings with fresh bakery products, salads, fruit juices and serious coffee. ◈ *Campo Pequeno 2A • Map C2*

9 CAMJAP café
The café and self-service restaurant at the Gulbenkian Foundation's modern art centre *(see p24)* has a reputation for quality and value. The museum's park is another draw. ◈ *Centro de Arte Moderna José Azeredo Perdigão, Rua Dr Nicolau Bettencourt • Map F1*

10 Pastelaria Versailles
Wonderful if slightly yellowed, this café and pastry shop has a grandiose interior, harassed brylcreemed waiters and worldly-wise elderly lady customers. ◈ *Avenida República 15A • Map F1*

Left **Casino Estoril** Right **Cascais Marina**

Lisbon Coast

‖TS RIVIERA-RIVALLING HEYDAY MAY BE A DISTANT MEMORY NOW, *but the varied coastline from the mouth of the Tejo to Europe's westernmost point has newer attractions too. Known locally as the* linha, *the coastal region has become one of Lisbon's most populous suburban zones – and yet it retains a laid-back holiday atmosphere. Above and behind it, Sintra's rock-strewn slopes and fragrant woods have a much more ancient ambience.*

View from Cabo da Roca

🔟 Sights

1. Estoril Casino
2. Monte Estoril
3. Cascais–Estoril Waterfront
4. Cascais Marina
5. Guincho
6. Cabo da Roca
7. Convento dos Capuchos
8. Monserrate
9. Colares
10. Sintra

Preceding pages **Palácio da Pena, rising above the wooded Parque da Pena, Sintra**

Cascais–Estoril waterfront

Estoril Casino
Large and rather loud in style, the entertainment heart of Estoril is more than just "Europe's biggest casino", with both gaming tables and slot machines. It has several good restaurants, an art gallery, a varied concert calendar, a glitzy disco, a theatre stage and titillating floor shows. The palm-lined park in front adds a welcome touch of old-world glamour.
🔊 *Praça José Teodoro dos Santos*
• *21 466 77 00* • *Open 3pm–3am daily*
• *Adm varies* • *www.casino-estoril.pt*

Monte Estoril
The ridge that separates Estoril from Cascais was the site of the earliest resort development, during the first half of the 20th century. It is now a captivating jumble of grand mansions, shopping arcades and apartment hotels – and still manages to be leafy and quiet in parts. Its railway station is reached by way of a tunnel under the busy *Marginal* coast road.

Cascais–Estoril Waterfront
Estoril and Cascais are linked by a promenade which runs just above the beach, but mostly out of sight of the coast road. By far the best walk in either resort, it is lined with small restaurants and bars and occasionally sprayed by Atlantic breakers.

Cascais Marina
Just beyond the centre of the town, and curving around the original fortress on the headland, Cascais Marina is a recent addition. Its 650 berths can accommodate yachts up to 36 m (118 ft) long, with a maximum draught of 6 m (20 ft). The many small shops and restaurants also attract a non-sailing crowd. Nearby are the large municipal park of Cascais, the Conde de Castro Guimarães Museum and the Coconuts nightclub *(see p102)*.
🔊 *Casa de São Bernardo* • *21 482 48 57*
• *Reception open 9am–7pm (6pm in winter)* • *www.marinacascais.pt*

Guincho
Still relatively undeveloped, the windswept coastline beyond Cascais, extending to Cabo da Roca, is exhilarating and scenic, particularly at Guincho. The beach of the same name is popular for surfing (although it's not recommended for beginners), and the broad sands are good for other beach sports as well as for brisk walks. When it's too windy to swim or sunbathe here, there are several smaller, more protected beaches on either side. Some of the best restaurants in the area lie along the Guincho road *(see p103)*.

Guincho

Convento dos Capuchos

Cabo da Roca

The westernmost point of mainland Europe is a suitably dramatic clifftop location marked by a lighthouse. There is also a quotation from Luís de Camões' epic poem *The Lusiads*, carved in stone. But beware: Cape Roca is subject to the climatic peculiarities of the whole Sintra region. Take a jumper, even if it's hot when you leave Cascais; temperatures can be 10 degrees lower here, and the winds strong. Collectors of memorabilia can buy a certificate to prove that they have walked on the continent's western extremity. There is a good café and restaurant, called O Moinho, near the turnoff from the Sintra road, and Ursa beach *(see p49)* lies just north of the point.

Convento dos Capuchos

Standing above Cabo da Roca, near Peninha *(see p102)*, this 16th-century Franciscan monastery is a striking example of monastic frugality, and thus a rarity among Portugal's generally opulent religious buildings. The Capuchin monks' cells are small and plain, hewn from rock and lined with cork against echoes and the cold. The minimal decoration is limited to communal areas such as the chapel, the refectory and the chapterhouse. The small fountain could almost be in a Buddhist forest retreat.
⊗ On road N247-3 • Open 9:30am–5pm daily (7pm in summer) • Adm charge

Monserrate

These lovely gardens, with their blend of natural and artificial elements, the exotic and the familiar, epitomize some of the essential characteristics of the Sintra region and its inhabitants. Just look at the artificial "ruin" in the lower garden – it might have been designed for Walt Disney's

---

Colares Wine

Once famous for its velvety, long-lived red wines made from the Ramisco grape – one of Europe's few survivors of the phylloxera plague – Colares seems now to be reduced to wine history. Wine is still made, but very little has any of the qualities associated with classic Colares. It seems that the costs of maintaining the old vines – and of planting new ones deep in the sand that protected them from the scourge of the vine louse – is too high.

The Jungle Book – or at the rolling lawns flanked by tropical trees, or the marvellous pastiche of the palace-pavilion *(see p27)*.

9 Colares

This pretty, peaceful village between Sintra and the sea gave its name to one of Portugal's most famous table wines, now made in only tiny amounts of variable quality. (Wine-lovers can visit the cooperative in Colares, at the beginning of the road to Praia das Maças, or go out to Azenhas do Mar and look up Paulo Bernardino da Costa, a stubborn producer.) All the same, it's well worth lingering in the older parts of Colares, shaded by plane trees with their peeling, mottled bark. Seek out the restaurant and tea salon Colares Velho in the church square, and soak up the old atmosphere of privilege edged by penury.

10 Sintra

To have seen the world and left out Sintra is not truly to have seen – thus goes, more or less, a Spanish saying. When you visit this ravishing hill-town, set on the northern slopes of the Serra, it's easy to understand why it was the preferred summer retreat of Portuguese kings *(see pp26–7)*.

Fonte Mourisca, Sintra

A Sintra Drive

Morning

🕐 Starting out from **Cascais**, drive along the Guincho coast towards Cabo da Roca (road N247). After Guincho beach, the road begins to climb. Follow the main road past the turning to Malveira da Serra. Turn off to the left for **Cabo da Roca** or, a tiny bit farther on, to the right for **Peninha** and **Convento dos Capuchos**. The latter choice offers opportunities for walks in the woods and views across the Serra; the former an invigorating lungful of sea air and the possibility of a drink at the **O Moinho** bar. Back on the main road, carry on towards **Colares** and stop there for lunch, taking the time to explore the village.

Afternoon

From Colares take the smaller road (N375 heading inland) towards Sintra, which will lead you past Eugaria and to **Monserrate**. Make an extended stop at Monserrate, giving yourself time to enjoy the gardens. The area above the parking lot outside the entrance is a popular picnic spot. Carry on along the lovely road that tunnels through the woods until you reach stately **Seteais**, where tea might be in order. A short distance further on you will come to **Quinta da Regaleira** – worth visiting for its gardens and esoterica – before you enter **Sintra** proper. Follow the road up, until you find parking above the main town, then walk down and do the sights or head straight to **Lawrence's** *(see p116)* for dinner. You can return to Cascais (and Lisbon) via the faster N9.

Left **Palácio and Parque da Pena** Right **Boca do Inferno**

Best of the Rest

1 Azenhas do Mar
Small houses huddle together in this cliff-top village that spills down towards a rock pool by the Atlantic ocean. With several restaurants, it is popular for Sunday lunch outings. ◎ N375

2 Parque da Pena
The paths in the park around the Palácio da Pena lead to the highest point in the Sintra hills – Cruz Alta, at 530 m (1,740 ft). ◎ N247-3 • Open 9:30am–6pm (7pm in summer) daily • Adm charge

3 Peninha
The small Capela de Nossa Senhora de Penha was built at the turn of the 17th century. In 1918 António Carvalho Monteiro, the millionaire owner of the Quinta da Regaleira (see p27), added a mock-fortified eagle's nest residence. ◎ N247

4 Museu do Conde de Castro Guimarães
This tower and grand villa on a small creek just beyond Cascais marina (see p99) are said to have been inspired by a painting. ◎ Avenida Rei Humberto II de Itália • 21 482 54 07 • Open 10am–5pm Tue–Sun • Adm charge

5 Fábrica da Pólvora
A gunpowder factory back in the 15th century, this is now a cultural and leisure centre. ◎ Estrada das Fontaínhas, Barcarena • 21 438 14 00 • Open 9am–5pm (6pm in summer) daily • Adm charge varies

6 Boca do Inferno
The rocky coastline beyond Cascais is full of crevices cut by the waves. The Mouth of Hell is a particularly deep one, where the waves roar in and then shoot up a vertical hole, creating a geyser-like jet of spray. ◎ Estrada da Boca do Inferno (N247-8)

7 Coconuts
Cascais' best-known disco, aka the Nuts Club, is located right on the rocky coastline, next to the Santa Maria lighthouse. There are indoor and outdoor bars and dance floors. ◎ Avenida Rei Humberto de Itália 7

8 Cascais Cultural Centre
Opened in 2000, after lengthy renovation of a 17th-century convent building, this cultural centre holds regular exhibitions and concerts. ◎ Avenida Rei Humberto II de Itália • 21 484 89 00 • Open 10am–6pm Tue–Sun • Adm charge varies

9 Golf courses
There are eight golf courses along the Lisbon coast. Most are good, but Penha Longa, between Cascais and Sintra, and Oitavos, in the Quinta da Marinha complex, stand out.

10 Autódromo do Estoril
The Formula One Portuguese Grand Prix was held at the Estoril racetrack between 1984 and 1996. Today it hosts MotoGP and A1 Grand Prix events, among others. ◎ N9, Alcabideche

For more on Sintra **See pp26-7**

Price Categories

For a three course meal for one with half a bottle of wine (or equivalent meal), taxes and extra charges.	€ under €15
	€€ €15–€20
	€€€ €20–€30
	€€€€ €30–€40
	€€€€€ over €40

Verbasco

🔟 Restaurants

1 Porto de Santa Maria
Occupying a low, modern building, overlooking the dramatic coastline near Guincho beach, is one of the country's top fish and seafood restaurants. ◎ *Estrada do Guincho • 21 487 02 40 • Closed Mon • €€€€€*

2 Estoril Mandarim
Part of the Casino complex in Estoril, Portugal's most luxurious Chinese restaurant is also its best. ◎ *Casino do Estoril • 21 466 72 70 • Closed Tue • €€€€*

3 Sawasdee, Cascais
One of two Thai restaurants in Cascais, this place is centrally located. It serves all the most popular dishes as well as performances of Thai dance and song. ◎ *Beco Esconso 11, Cascais • 21 484 79 67 • Tue–Sun L only • €€€*

4 Dom Grelhas, Cascais
Located in Casa da Guia, a gated, cliff-side collection of restaurants and small shops, Dom Grelhas specializes in grilled meat and fish. Meals are accompanied by wide views of the sea. ◎ *Casa da Guia, Estrada do Guincho • 21 483 99 67 • €€€*

5 Fortaleza do Guincho
Magnificently sited in a 17th-century fortress on the Guincho coast, this is a fine restaurant with a modern French menu that makes good use of Portuguese ingredients. ◎ *Estrada do Guincho • 21 487 04 91 • €€€€€*

6 O Pereira, Cascais
This small, friendly restaurant serves hearty Portuguese food, prepared in a timeless way. ◎ *Rua da Bela Vista 92, Cascais • 21 483 12 15 • Closed Thu • €€*

7 Verbasco, Cascais
Sophisticated modern cuisine is served here in the airy clubhouse of the Oitavos golf course at Quinta da Marinha. ◎ *Quinta da Marinha Oitavos Golf • 21 486 06 06 • Closed Sun D, Mon L • €€€€€*

8 La Villa, Estoril
In a landmark building with a tower by the beach at Estoril, this luxurious restaurant is on two floors. Downstairs the food is modern Mediterranean; upstairs there is a sushi bar and terrace. ◎ *Praia do Tamariz • 21 468 00 33 • Closed Mon • €€€€*

9 Bar das Avencas
Seemingly hanging off the cliff above a quiet beach, this simple but well-designed bar serves sandwiches, salads and hamburgers, as well as a couple of other unfussy cooked dishes. ◎ *Avenida Marginal (Parede) • 21 457 27 17 • Closed Tue in winter • €*

10 Buchanan's, Cascais
With views over Cascais bay from the terrace, this ambitious restaurant has an eclectic modern menu that includes interesting vegetarian options. ◎ *Travessa da Alfarrobeira • 21 484 75 90 • €€€€*

Both Porto de Santa Maria and Fortaleza do Guincho have one Michelin star.

STREETSMART

LISBON'S TOP 10

Left **Tourist tram** Centre **Metro sign** Right **Lisbon taxi**

🔟 Getting to and around Lisbon

1 Airport
Lisbon's Portela airport has two terminals – one for domestic flights only. Transfers to the centre, 7 km (4 miles) away, cost €8–12 by taxi. Allow 20–30 minutes, or twice that during the rush hour.

2 Railway Stations
Santa Apolónia station, on Lisbon's eastern waterfront, is the terminus for trains from Madrid and the north of Portugal. Trains from the south and east arrive at Barreiro on the Tejo, from where a ferry makes the crossing to Terreiro do Paço.

3 Arriving by Road
From the south and east, drivers arrive on the A2 motorway. The A12 branches off the A2 just after Setúbal and leads to the 17-km (11-mile) Vasco da Gama bridge, which is the best approach for the north and east of the city. For the centre and west, you should stay on the A2 and cross on the 25 de Abril suspension bridge. Arrival from the north is on the A1.

4 Trams and Funiculars
Trams and funiculars are Lisbon's most appealing forms of public transport, but not its most efficient. The most useful trams for seeing the city are the 28 and the 25. The 15 runs on a modern line from Praça da Figueira to Belém and Algés and is the only

fast service. Funiculars carry weary *lisboetas* up three of the city's hills.

5 Metro and Buses
Covering most of the city except the west, the metro is the fastest way of getting around. Trains run from 6:30am to 1am. Tickets for buses are the same as for trams and funiculars. They may be bought on boarding or in advance at Carris booths.

6 Ferries
The busiest crossings over the Tejo, for both cars and passengers, are at Terreiro do Paço and Cais do Sodré. Ferries leave Belém for Porto Brandão and Trafaria, which have bus services to the Caparica coast.

7 Organized Tours
The Transtejo ferry company operates a daily river cruise from Terreiro do Paço from 1st April–31st October, which leaves at 3pm and returns at around 5:30pm. Carris Lisbon tours, on open-top double-decker buses and tourist trams, depart from Praça do Comércio throughout the day. They also operate a river cruise from the Alcântara docks at 4pm from Tuesday to Saturday.

8 Taxis
Cream or black-and-green Lisbon taxis may be hailed, caught at ranks or ordered by phone. Fares are low for Europe.

Tourist taxis are dark and unmarked except for a green "A" on the bumper. They cost more and may line up at the airport taxi rank. Tipping is common.

9 Lisbon Coast Trains
Trains to Estoril and Cascais depart from the riverside Cais do Sodré station. Some terminate at Oeiras along the way. Trains to Sintra depart from Rossio and Entrecampos stations.

10 Walking
Lisbon is a safe city best explored on foot. Some of its hills are steep and the cobbled pavements get slippery in rain.

Transport

Airport
21 841 37 00 • www.ana-aeroportos.pt

Buses, Trams and Funicular
www.carris.pt

Ferries
210 422 400
• www.transtejo.pt

Metro
www.metrolisboa.pt

Taxis
Autocoope: 21 793 27 56 • Retalis Radio Taxis: 21 811 90 00
• Teletáxis: 21 811 11 00

Trains
• General train info: 808 208 208; 351 213 815 990 calls from overseas (line open 7am–11pm)
• www.cp.pt

Preceding pages **View of Praça Dom Pedro IV**

Left *Agenda Cultural* listings magazine Right Lisboa Welcome Centre

TOP 10 General Information

1 When to Go
Summer is, of course, high season. After August, things calm down, while the sea is as warm as it ever gets. Later autumn can be very pleasant; December to February usually brings damp and chilly weather. Early spring is one of the best times to make your visit.

2 Bookings
Book hotels well ahead for stays in June, July and August. Expect mid- to top-range hotels in central Lisbon, Cascais and Estoril to be busy all year round. You may be asked for written confirmation, with a credit card number, by fax or e-mail.

3 Visas
EU nationals with a valid passport or identity card may stay for six months before needing a residence permit. Most non-EU nationals can stay for 90 days without a visa. Regulations are subject to change, so check with a Portuguese embassy or consulate before your trip.

4 Customs
Limits on what EU citizens may import for personal use are set high, though weapons, plants and perishable foods are not permitted.

5 Travelling with Children
Lisbon may not have kneeling buses or baby-care facilities at every turn, and its pavements require all-terrain push-chairs, but most *lisboetas* have an effusive love of children. Only the very smartest restaurants frown on toddler guests, and making noise is a virtue, not a sin.

6 Lisboa Welcome Center
Lisbon's tourist office is an association with more than 400 paying members. As a result it has a corporate feel and usually offers snappy service, but its members tend to be promoted at the expense of non-members. ◉ *Rua do Arsenal 15 • Map M6 • 21 031 27 00 • www.atl-turismolisboa.pt*

7 Websites
Try www. visitportugal.com or www.portugaltravelguide.com for tourist advice; www.maisturismo.pt for hotel listings; www. lifecooler.com for restaurant and bar listings (though it is in Portuguese); and www.portugalvirtual.pt for general information.

8 Listings Publications
Agenda Cultural is a monthly events and listings mini-magazine. It covers just about everything, is generally accurate – and can be picked up for free at many hotel receptions and tourist attractions. The tourist association's monthly *Follow Me Lisboa* has the fullest coverage of events in English. A round up of weekly events can also be viewed at the *le cool* website. ◉ *www. lecool.com/lisboa*

9 English-language Newspapers
If you want an English-language newspaper try *The Portugal News* or *The Portugal Resident*, both published in the Algarve and aimed at expats, but with some useful information for visitors.

10 Public Holidays
Public holidays are frequent and include Dia de Santo António, for the city's patron saint (13 Jun).

Embassies

Australian Embassy
Avda da Liberdade 200, 2E • Map F3 • 21 310 15 00

Canadian Embassy
Avda da Liberdade 196–200, 3 • Map F3 • 21 316 46 00

Indian Embassy
R Pero da Covilhã 16 • Map A5 • 21 304 10 90

Irish Embassy
R da Imprensa à Estrela 1, 4 • Map E4 • 21 392 94 40

UK Embassy
R de São Bernardo 33 • Map E4 • 21 392 40 00

US Embassy
Avda das Forças Armadas • Map C2 • 21 727 33 00

Most museums and monuments are closed on Mondays.

Left **Police** Centre **Pharmacy sign** Right **Heavy Lisbon traffic**

Health and Security

1 Health Precautions
Visitors to Portugal do not need vaccinations or to take any other health precautions ahead of their trip. Once here, a good suntan lotion is a must, particularly if you are fair-skinned. Tap water is safe, but tastes of chlorine.

2 Beach Safety
Beware of currents and undertow in the sea, and don't ignore the safety flags: red – no going in the sea; yellow – no swimming; green – all clear. Nasty stings in shallow water may be from poisonous scorpion fish (peixe-aranha) buried in the sand. The temporary intense pain and swelling can be alleviated by applying heat to the area; alternatively seek the help of a lifeguard.

3 Pharmacies
Pharmacies are marked by a green cross. Pharmacy staff often dispense advice as well as medication. A closed pharmacy will have a sign in its window telling you which local one is open.

4 Medical Treatment
EU citizens are entitled to free or sub-sidized medical treatment if they have a European Health Insurance Card with them (the replacement for the E111). If you don't have the card, but pay into your country's social security system, the cost of treatment can be claimed back later, at risk of bureaucratic hassle. Private health insurance is likely to lead to more efficient treatment.

5 Security
Lisbon remains a safe city by the standards of most European capitals. Visitors should be wary of pickpockets – particularly on public transport – and of leaving valuables in hired cars. More serious crime is mostly confined to certain outlying areas, but walking alone at night through districts with little nocturnal activity – such as the Baixa – is not recommended.

6 Police
The PSP (Polícia de Segurança Pública) has a benevolent, if slightly inefficient, image. There is a police station for tourists on Restauradores, next to the national tourist office in Palácio Foz. The GNR (National Guard) has a tougher reputation.

7 Traffic
Foreigners are often incensed by aggressive and dangerous Portuguese driving habits.

8 Women Travellers
By southern European standards, Portuguese men are not that predatory. However, even pairs or small groups of women may be hassled on beaches and in clubs. It is often more effective to confront the pest loudly than to ignore him, particularly if there are other people around.

9 Disabled Access
Disabled people will find that the metro is the most accessible form of public transport. Lisbon is hilly and has narrow cobbled pavements with parked cars often blocking the way. Most new public buildings offer good disabled access; a lack of facilities elsewhere is often compensated for by a willingness to help.

10 Disabled Organizations
INR (Instituto Nacional para a Reabilitação) deals with rights of disabled people and its website has an English-language section. CNAD provides information on disabled services, while Adaptacar rents modified vehicles.

Useful Organizations

Ambulance
112 (emergency); or contact nearest hospital

CNAD
21 859 53 32

INR
21 792 95 00
• www.inr.pt

Police
GNR: 112 (emergency)
• PSP: 21 342 16 34 (Restauradores)
• Tourism Police: 21 342 16 34

Left **Bar area, NetCenter Café** Centre **Post office** Right **Newspaper and magazine stand**

TOP 10 Banking and Communications

Currency
Euros are the currency in Portugal. Coins are frequently used, even the smallest denominations. Large-value notes are quite rare and may be viewed with suspicion.

Credit Cards
Major credit cards, with the exception of American Express, are widely accepted in bigger hotels, shops, restaurants and bars.

Cash Dispensers
Known as Multibanco in Lisbon, cash dispensers are ubiquitous. Most now accept debit and credit cards from the major card companies, but transaction charges apply.

Changing Money
Banks are the easiest places to use if you want to change money and charges don't vary widely. For the less common currencies, and after banking hours, seek out one of the Forex services in Rossio or one of the city's few money-changing machines, such as the one opposite the Avenida Palace hotel *(see p112)*.

Post Offices
Correios (post offices) are dotted around the city, but for buying stamps use the red, coin-operated dispensers as this will save you joining lengthy queues. First-class mail is known as *correio azul*. The main post office on Restauradores is open at weekends; others operate 9am to 6pm on weekdays.

Telephones
There are three mobile operators: TMN (with numbers beginning 96), Vodafone (91) and Optimus (93). Coverage is good. Though rarer now, there are still public phones in Lisbon. With a phone card (available from post offices, newsagents, tobacconists and Portugal Telecom shops), they can be the cheapest option. There are fewer coin-operated phones, and they are less economical. All numbers within the country have nine digits. To call abroad, dial 00 and the country code first.

Internet Cafés and Wi-Fi Hotspots
Internet cafés in three main shopping centres – Columbo, Monumental and Vasco da Gama – are open from 10am to midnight seven days a week. Internet access is also available at PostNet and at Forum Picoas opposite the Sheraton *(see p115)*. Most of these also offer Wi-Fi access. Other wireless hotspots are hotels, post offices, petrol stations and the airport. 🌐 *NetCenter Cafe. Com: Rua do Diário de Notícias 157–9, Bairro Alto. Map K4 • K@netpoint: Columbo (opposite Benfica's Stadium of Light) • PostNet: Rua Braamcamp 9, near Marquês Pombal.*

Map F3 • *Forum Picoas: Portugal Telecom building, Rua Tomás Ribeiro. Map F2*

Newspapers and Magazines
Local dailies include *Público* and *Diário de Notícias*, both of which carry cinema listings.

Radio and TV
There is plenty of choice in music stations. Capital (100.8FM), RFM (93.2) and Antena 3 (100.3) are all middle of the road. Oxigénio (102.6), Mix (103) and Orbital (101.9) are more dance oriented. Marginal (98.1), Baía (98.7) and África (101.5) are mostly easy listening, while Antena 2 (94.4) is classical. The state-owned TV company is RTP: RTP 1 is commercial, with various sub-channels, and RTP 2 is culturally oriented. SIC, operating a plethora of channels, and TVI are private broadcasters. In Portugal foreign-language films are subtitled, not dubbed. Most hotels offer ample cable choice.

Speaking to the Locals
Portuguese can be challenging to the ear and those nasal endings hard to emulate, but no one will disapprove if you try. *Lisboetas* are proud of their language and mostly generous in interpreting it. Spanish is widely understood and so is English.

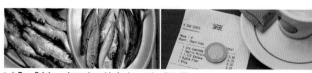

Left **Raw fish brought to the table for inspection** Right **Tipping**

📑10 Eating, Lodging and Shopping

1 Reservations
It is always better to book a restaurant table in advance, though usually only necessary for dinner, weekend lunches and at the most popular places. A few restaurants do not take reservations, in which case arrive before 8pm to avoid a wait.

2 Meal Times
The Portuguese do not eat as late as the Spanish. Most restaurants open between 7am and 8pm and close between 11pm and midnight. Lunch kicks off at around 1–2pm, and gets later and longer at weekends. During the week, a late lunch is a good way of avoiding a wait; for dinner, an early start has the same result.

3 Unrequested Appetizers
To varying degrees, all Portuguese restaurants place a selection of appetizers – usually cheeses, olives, bread and perhaps ham or salami – on the table before you order anything. These are often delicious, but they are not free. In many cheaper restaurants, they may end up doubling the cost of the meal. If you don't want to be tempted, just ask the waiter to remove them.

4 Choosing Dishes
Many restaurants have the laudable policy of displaying their meat and fish in glass-fronted refrigerators, allowing you to judge their quality and freshness. With fish, waiters will often bring the raw fish to the table for inspection. If you are in a hurry, or just hungry, order dishes listed as *pratos do dia*, dishes of the day. In general, fish is served with boiled potatoes and meat with chips and sometimes rice. However, this habit can be broken at the customer's request.

5 Portion Sizes
Traditional restaurants – and Lisbon still has many in this category – serve portions calculated to meet the calorie requirements of manual labourers rather than office workers or weight-conscious visitors. There is an established system of half portions – known as *meia dose* – that operates particularly at lunchtime. You get less food for your euros at more up-to-date restaurants, which serve smaller portions.

6 Tipping
A five to ten per cent tip is regarded as fairly generous after a meal in a restaurant. There is no obligation, and at lunch, in cafés or at bar counters, tips are much smaller.

7 Hotel Gradings
Hotels are graded with one to five stars, based on a fixed set of criteria covering most aspects of comfort. *Pensões* are classified from 3rd (lowest) to 1st (highest) grade, while the most luxurious are *albergaria*. Bear in mind that a one-, two- or even three-star hotel will be more basic than the top categories of *pensão*.

8 Hotel Prices
Most hotels' prices vary considerably over the year, and the margin for bargaining is quite large in Lisbon's now slightly over-supplied hotel market. It is also worth remembering that some of the business hotels regard summer as their low season.

9 Shop Hours
Shop hours are from 9am to 1pm and 2pm or 3pm to 7pm on weekdays. On Saturdays, shops are generally open until lunchtime and they close all day Sunday. The large shopping centres are an exception; many of their outlets are open through-out the day, until 10pm or 11pm, all week.

10 Bargaining
Bargaining is not common practice in shops, and attempts may be frowned upon – even when prices abundantly suggest it, as in antiques shops. Small "discounts" may sometimes be obtained for nebulous reasons, but the real bargaining is reserved for the casual market trade.

Left **Pretty but slippery cobbled pavement** Right **A rare port advertisement**

TOP 10 Things to Avoid

1 Rush Hour
The rush hour is roughly between 8:30am and 10am in the morning and 6pm and 8pm in the evening. While the trains are packed, the metro is much less affected. At peak times, it is best to allow about 40 minutes for the taxi ride to the airport from the centre.

2 Sintra at Weekends
Sintra (see pp26–7) suffers more than most from the weekend onslaught. Tour buses clog the roads and obscure the views, the queues to the main sights seem interminable, and cafés and restaurants are subject to frenzied rushes. In the week it is a different place – but bear in mind that the National Palace is closed on Wednesdays.

3 Driving in the City
Driving in Lisbon is generally unnecessary for visitors: distances are not huge, public transport covers most of the city and taxis are fairly cheap. Navigating its streets can be challenging – and Portuguese patience evaporates behind the wheel. Besides, the city is best discovered and enjoyed on foot. If you must drive, weekends are quieter than weekdays.

4 Thin-soled Shoes
Lisbon's pretty cobbled pavements are not even and get lethally slippery as soon as it starts to rain. If you intend to walk further than to the local restaurant, wear properly supportive, rubber-soled shoes.

5 Dog-fouled Pavements
The city's pavements can also be real minefields of dog mess, particularly in residential areas. Dog owners are only gradually starting to clean up after their pets. A few moped dog-mess hoovers are sporadically deployed.

6 Eating out on Sundays
A considerable proportion of Lisbon restaurants do not open on Sundays – and most of those that do close on Mondays instead. On either of these days, it is best to check with the restaurant before turning up.

7 *Fado* for Tourists
Fado represents a tourist obligation in Lisbon, which means that there is a market for packaging it in cost-effective ways. Culture loses on this, though, as does the experience you take away. Approach *fado* through the less grand *fado vadio* venues, then move on to the better fado restaurants (see p43) if you feel smitten by it.

8 Warmed Coffee
Lisbon is a city that takes its coffee seriously, but cafés indulge in one bad habit: keeping coffee warm for making the Portuguese equivalent of a *latte*, known as a *galão* and served in a tall glass. Ask for a *galão de máquina* to ensure that a freshly-made jet of coffee goes into yours.

9 Chip-fat Smell
Chips are a staple of Portuguese restaurants, and the deep-fat fryer is switched on throughout the day in most of them. In small, badly ventilated restaurants – that is, the majority – this may not be noticeable or particularly unpleasant at the time, but after leaving you will carry a strong smell of burnt deep-frying oil in your clothes. Some counter-measures include wearing a leather jacket; sitting outside; going to a sushi restaurant; or airing your clothes on your hotel balcony.

10 Port in the Wrong Places
It surprises many visitors that they don't see the Portuguese quaffing port in bars. Port is in fact mostly drunk at home, on special occasions. This means that most bars do not stock it, or if they do, that it is likely to be cheap, nasty and over-oxidized. Gourmet restaurants will always be serious about their port; alternatively you can head for the Port Wine Institute or Enoteca (see p95).

A ban on smoking in public places, introduced in January 2008, has been relaxed to allow smoking in places with ventilation.

111

Left **Pestana Palace** Right **Lisboa Regency**

TOP 10 Luxury Hotels

Ritz Four Seasons
Few hotels can better this one for service. There may be luxury hotels in more attractive locations (though the roof-top running track is far removed from the traffic below) and with more characterful interiors (but take a look at the spa) – yet the Ritz is absolutely there for its guests. 🅢 *Rua Rodrigo da Fonseca 88 • Map F3 • 21 381 14 00 • www.four seasons.com/lisbon • €€€€€*

Lapa Palace
Opulent and eclectic in its decor, this is now an established jewel in Lisbon's hotel crown. The location is quiet, but quite a walk from the centre. 🅢 *Rua do Pau da Bandeira 4 • Map E5 • 21 394 94 94 • www. lapapalace.com • €€€€€*

Pestana Palace
One of the newest of Lisbon's top-rated hotels occupies a marvellously restored 19th-century palace with extensions framing the garden. It is located between central Lisbon and Belém. 🅢 *Rua Jau 54 • Map G5 • 21 361 56 00 • www. pestana.com • €€€€€*

Avenida Palace
The doyen of the city's luxury hotels has a colourful history going back to the early 20th century. Since its major restoration a few years ago, purists have found it all a bit too mock-Belle

Époque, but the location and atmosphere are hard to beat. 🅢 *Rua 1° de Dezembro 123 • Map L3 • 21 321 81 00 • www.hotel-avenida-palace.pt • €€€€*

Tivoli Lisboa
After half a century, Lisbon's original Tivoli hotel has earned the right to be called a classic. The vast lobby is an arcaded piazza that succeeds in being simultaneously grand and cosy. Another major attraction is the roof-top grill, with the views that most rooms lack. 🅢 *Avenida da Liberdade 185 • Map K1 • 21 319 89 00 • www. tivolihotels.com • €€€€€*

Altis
All the features and comforts of its five-star rating are found here at a competitive price, which makes up for the nondescript interior. Prices are open to negotiation; summer is low season at this mainly business hotel. 🅢 *Rua Castilho 11 • Map F3 • 21 310 60 00 • www. altishotels.com • €€€€*

Real Palácio
Old and new blend easily here. A restored private palace, dating in its oldest parts back to the 17th century, adjoins a modern hotel building. The latter is filled with reproduction furnishings, but it is the palace, with its small patio, archways and tiled stairwells, that is the highlight. 🅢 *Rua*

Tomás Ribeiro • Map F2 • 21 319 95 00 • www. hoteisreal.com • €€€€€

Tiara Park Atlantic Lisboa
In a modern building overlooking the Eduardo VII park, this is first and foremost a business hotel: comfortable, practical and professional. Some rooms on the higher floors have great views. 🅢 *Rua Castilho 149 • Map F2 • 21 381 87 00 • www.tiara-hotels.com • €€€€€*

Heritage Av Liberdade
A recent addition to the small Heritage hotel group, this centrally located hotel is housed in a restored late 18th-century building. It is a showcase for Portuguese interior designer Miguel Câncio Martins, who mixes modernity with an oriental simplicity and warmth. 🅢 *Avenida da Liberdade 28 • Map F3 • 21 340 40 40 • www. heritage.pt • €€€€*

Lisboa Regency Chiado
This medium-sized hotel has a privileged location. Some rooms have private verandas that look out over the Baixa to Castelo de São Jorge *(see pp8–9)*, and down to the river. There is also a large veranda for all guests to enjoy. 🅢 *Rua Nova do Almada 114 • Map L4 • 21 325 61 00 • www.regency-hotels-resorts.com • €€€€*

Note: Unless otherwise stated, all hotels accept credit cards and have en-suite bathrooms and air conditioning

Duas Nações

Budget Hotels

Florescente
This place feels considerably more posh than the price suggests. It is also neater and cleaner than most of the competition. Dead-central location, parking facilities and free Wi-Fi Internet access enhance the good value that it offers. ⊗ Rua Portas de Santo Antão 99 • Map L2 • 21 342 66 09 • www.residencial florescente.com • €€

Londres
Longtime favourite of budget travellers, the Londres has recently gone upmarket. Cheaper rooms are still available – but the best one is at the top, overlooking Bairro Alto's warren of streets. ⊗ Rua Dom Pedro V 53, 2 • Map K2 • 21 346 22 03 • no air con • www.pensao londres.com.pt • €€

Alegria
The name Alegria, which translates as "joy", has often been said to refer to the girls of easy virtue who sometimes still venture to these parts – though there is now a police station next door. Conveniently located off the main drag but near the action, it offers fairly basic lodgings. ⊗ Praça da Alegria 12 • Map K2 • 21 322 06 70 • www.alegrianet.com • €

Horizonte
This comfortable, well-equipped, value-for-money pensão is in Lisbon's mid-

town, near the Eduardo VII park and a short walk from the Gulbenkian (see pp24–5) and the Corte Inglês department store (see p94). ⊗ Avenida António Augusto de Aguiar 42 • Map F2 • 21 353 95 26 • www.hotelhorizonte. com • €

Princesa
The setting for this cheap and comfortable pensão is a fairly central, but non-touristy part of the city. Downtown Lisbon is a lengthy downhill walk away; guests might want to return via the Elevador do Lavra (see p66) and the Psi café-restaurant (see p95). Some rooms can be noisy. ⊗ Rua Gomes Freire 130 • Map G3 • 21 319 30 70 • www.residencial- princesa.pt • €

Globo
Located on a quiet Bairro Alto street, this basic and friendly pensão is an economical choice. The Olivier restaurant (see p77) is in the same street. ⊗ Rua do Teixeira 37 • Map K3 • 21 346 22 79 • no air con, no credit cards • www.cb2web. com/globo • €

Alcantarense
Well placed for club-life in the Alcântara and Docas areas, this simple pensão caters mainly to business clients on a budget – some of the 17 rooms are always taken by long-term guests. For

short stays, rooms can be had for as little as €35 a night. ⊗ Rua Vieira da Silva 119, 1D • Map D5 • 21 396 65 52 • no air con, no CC • €

Ibérica
This is almost as cheap as it gets if you want your own room and a central location – right in the heart of things in this case. Your fellow guests are likely to be on a tight budget. A frugal place it may be, but not in any way threatening. ⊗ Praça da Figueira 10, 2 • Map M3 • 21 886 57 81 • no en-suite, no air con, no CC • €

Duas Nações
With a sometimes startling interior, but a good-natured atmosphere, this upmarket pensão occupies a grand old building in the Baixa. It is well-sited for compulsive shoppers, standing on a corner with the pedestrianized Rua Augusta. ⊗ Rua da Vitória 41 • Map M4 • 21 346 07 10 • no air con • www.duasnacoes. com • €€

Lar do Areeiro
Located north of the centre, this extremely comfortable pensão is near the Roma shopping district (see p40), the Bela Vista park (see p94) and the airport. ⊗ Praça Francisco Sá Carneiro 4 • Map G1 • 21 849 31 50 • www.residen- cialardo areeiro.com • €€

Prices are less negotiable in budget hotels; sometimes a haggle in a more expensive hotel will lead to the same price as a budget option.

Left **Bairro Alto** Right **York House**

Character Hotels

Palácio Belmonte
Ten suites, each with its own character, occupy the city's oldest private palace, sumptuously restored with a near-manic attention to detail, craftsmanship and historical authenticity. Buttressed on one side by Castelo de São Jorge (see pp8–9), the Belmonte offers fine views from its terraces and a small pool hidden from the public eye. The place is a dream, costing real money. ◊ Pátio Dom Fradique • Map P4 • 21 881 66 00 • www.palacio belmonte.com • €€€€€

Bairro Alto
Set in an attractively restored 18th-century building in Praça de Camões, in the heart of Lisbon, this hotel delivers luxury with style. ◊ Praça Luís de Camões 2 • Map K4 • 21 340 82 88 • www. bairroaltohotel.com • €€€€€

Solar do Castelo
Once the kitchens of the original Alcáçovas Palace in Castelo de São Jorge (see pp8–9), then converted into a private palace in the 18th century, this is now a cosy, eclectically furnished boutique hotel around a small courtyard. ◊ Rua das Cozinhas 2 • Map N3 • 21 880 60 50 • www.heritage.pt • €€€€

Quinta Nova da Conceição
This 18th-century summer residence – it was then far beyond the limits of

the city – is still owned by the same family and has an atmosphere few character hotels can match. Book early, as there are only three rooms. ◊ Rua Cidade de Rabat 5 • Map B2 • 21 778 00 91 • www.quintanova conceicao.com • €€€

York House
A former 17th-century convent, turned into a boarding house by two Yorkshire women in the 19th century. Graham Greene stayed here, when rates were lower and the furnishings less stylish. The place hasn't lost its character – the dark corridors could come from a story by Borges. ◊ Rua das Janelas Verdes 32 • Map E5 • 21 396 24 35 • www.yorkhouselisboa. com • €€€€

Olissippo Castelo
Beautifully located beneath Castelo de São Jorge, with views across the city, this is the pride of the small Olissippo hotels group. It provides extreme comfort in light, airy, textile-rich rooms. ◊ Rua Costa do Castelo 112–26 • Map N3 • 21 882 01 90 • www. olissippohotels.com • €€€€

Metropole
Decorated with real Art-Nouveau pieces as well as reproductions, the Metropole has a genuine feel and a superb central location overlooking Rossio. As part of the

Almeida chain, it has the bonus of offering prized wines from the Bussaco Palace Hotel. ◊ Praça Dom Pedro IV (Rossio) 30 • Map L3 • 21 321 90 30 • www. almeidahotels.com • €€€

Britânia
Well placed in a quiet street just off Avenida da Liberdade, the Britânia is a gem with a style all its own. Housed in a 1940s building, it combines wood and marble in its Art-Deco design and goes easy on the textiles. ◊ Rua Rodrigues Sampaio 17 • Map F3 • 21 315 50 16 • www.heritage.pt • €€€€

Casa de São Mamede
This atmospheric if somewhat hushed pensão has a good location slightly off the main tourist track. Set in a grand 18th-century residence, it gives a taste of an older Lisbon. ◊ Rua da Escola Politécnica 159 • Map F3 • 21 396 31 66 • No credit cards • www. saomamede.web.pt • €€

Pousada Dona Maria I, Queluz
The closest pousada to central Lisbon occupies an annexe of the Palácio de Quelu (see pp22–3) and has a renowned restaurant. Plush but light-toned, it has the air of an haut-bourgeois late 19th-century summer residence. ◊ Largo do Palácio Nacional de Queluz • Map A1 • 21 435 61 58 • www.pousadas.pt • €€€€

Note: Unless otherwise stated, all hotels accept credit cards and have en-suite bathrooms and air conditioning

Solar dos Mouros

Price Categories

For a standard, double room per night (with breakfast if included), taxes and extra charges.

€	under €50
€€	€50–100
€€€	€100–€175
€€€€	€175–€250
€€€€€	over €250

Rooms with a View

1 Albergaria Senhora do Monte

Set on one of Lisbon's highest hills, this relatively plain hotel boasts some of the city's best views. It's a quiet perch for the walking, atmosphere-absorbing visitor. ⊗ *Calçada do Monte 39 • Map P1 • 21 886 60 02 • www.maisturismo.pt/sramonte • €€€*

2 Sheraton

A landmark on the city's modest skyline, the Sheraton has beautiful views from its rather 1970s interior. A business hotel, it offers five-star comfort at reasonable rates and a panoramic roof-top restaurant. ⊗ *Rua Latino Coelho 1 • Map F2 • 21 312 00 00 • www.sheraton.com • €€€€*

3 Dom Pedro

This lofty glass pile in the Amoreiras business and shopping district features traditional, textile-heavy luxury – with the exception of some of the suites. Views from almost every room are stunning. ⊗ *Avenida Engenheiro Duarte Pacheco 24 • Map E3 • 21 389 66 00 • www.dompedro.com • €€€€€*

4 Mundial

Superbly located in downtown Lisbon, the eight-floor Mundial has views across the Baixa and up towards the castle. Comfortable rooms serve their purpose and have large windows that open:

a potential hazard for children. The roof-top restaurant is popular with local politicians. ⊗ *Praça Martim Moniz 2• Map M3 • 21 884 20 00 • www.hotel-mundial.pt • €€€*

5 Eduardo VII

Just off the park of the same name (and the busy Marquês de Pombal roundabout), the Best Western Eduardo VII offers good value and great views from many of its pleasant, if small, rooms. A panoramic restaurant and a clubby bar complete the picture. ⊗ *Avenida Fontes Pereira de Melo 5 • Map F2 • 21 356 88 00 • www.hoteleduardovii.pt • €€€*

6 Tryp Oriente

This purpose-built hotel by Parque das Nações (see pp16–17) provides modern facilities, plus views of the wide Tejo estuary from light, airy rooms. The location gives easy access to the airport. It is part of the Sol Meliá chain. ⊗ *Avenida Dom João II • Map C1 • 21 893 00 00 • www.tryporiente.solmelia.com • €€€*

7 NH Liberdade

Decorated in the sober, modern style of the Spanish NH chain, this sophisticated hotel has a roof-top swimming pool with superb vistas. Rooms on the higher floors have good views of the Avenida. ⊗ *Avenida da Liberdade 180B • Map K1*

• 21 351 40 60 • www.nh-hotels.com • €€€€

8 13 da Sorte

Most rooms in this good-value *pensão* near Avenida da Liberdade have nice views over the Jardim Botânico (see p81) and Parque Mayer, the old vaudeville park, site of a shelved project for a Frank Gehry-designed casino. ⊗ *Rua do Salitre 13 • Map K1 • 21 353 97 46 • www.trezedasorte.no.sapo.pt • €*

9 Ninho das Águias

This has to be one of the city's most attractive *pensões*, for the wonderful old building itself, its large communal terrace, its turret, its location just below the castle walls and the views (which are, however, away from the river). Rooms are basic, though, and it's a long climb up a spiral staircase to get here. ⊗ *Rua Costa do Castelo 74 • Map N3 • 21 885 40 70 • no en-suite, no air con, no credit cards • €*

10 Solar dos Mouros

Located on the remains of one of the Moorish-era gates to Castelo de São Jorge, this small hotel has simply but tastefully decorated rooms. Contemporary art from the owner's private collection features prominently, as do views of the city and the river. ⊗ *Rua do Milagre de Santo António 6 • Map N4 • 21 885 49 40 • www.solardosmouros.com • €€€€*

For some of Lisbon's many viewing points **See pp36–7**

Left **Seteais Palace, near Sintra** Right **Fortaleza do Guincho**

🔟 Lisbon Coast Hotels

1 Albatroz
Central Cascais' most characterful hotel has a to-die-for location on a promontory with sandy beaches to either side. The main building typifies the summer villas built here for aristocrats in the 19th century. The Italianate Albatroz Palace across the street is also part of the hotel. 🕲 *Rua Frederico Arouca 100, Cascais • 21 484 73 80 • www. albatroz hotels.com • €€€€€*

2 Casa da Pérgola
With its two-tone mansard roof, curving eaves and tiled window surrounds, this elegant bed and breakfast in central Cascais is unmistakable. The garden is also dazzling. 🕲 *Avenida Valbom 13, Cascais • 21 484 00 40 • www.pergolahouse. com • €€€*

3 Palácio Estoril
Still with a whiff of Estoril's heyday as a glamorous resort, the Palácio was built in the 1930s and former guests range from royalty to spies. Its enduring grandeur is attested by its interiors and service. 🕲 *Rua Particular, Estoril • 21 464 80 00 • www.palacio estorilhotel.com • €€€€€*

4 Farol Design
Within an extended villa overlooking the sea, this modern luxury hotel has interiors designed by top names in Portuguese fashion. For all the design hype, the main attraction is that some rooms have floor-to-ceiling windows, giving you the feeling of crawling into bed at sea. 🕲 *Avenida Rei Humberto II de Itália 7, Cascais • 21 482 34 90 • www.farol.com.pt • €€€€€*

5 Senhora da Guia
Just outside central Cascais and a chip away from the Quinta da Marinha golf course, this hotel embodies civilized luxury with a slightly English touch. It has a salt-water pool. 🕲 *Estrada do Guincho, Cascais • 21 486 92 39 • www. senhora daguia.com • €€€€€*

6 Palácio Seteais
One of the many gems of the Sintra region, this palatial hotel was built for a Dutch diplomat in 1787; its Neo-Classical façade and triumphal arch were added later. Now part of the Tivoli chain, it offers the usual luxuries and an inimitable atmosphere. 🕲 *Rua Barbosa du Bocage 8–10, Sintra • 21 923 32 00 • www. tivoli hotels.com • €€€€€*

7 Lawrence's
This charming small hotel is at the edge of Sintra town. Some of its individually furnished rooms are named after famous writer guests, among them Lord Byron. Owned by an affable Dutch couple, it has a restaurant that is run with a real passion. 🕲 *Rua Consiglieri Pedroso 38–40, Sintra • 21 910 55 00 • www.lawrenceshotel. com • €€€€*

8 Quinta da Capela
Low, simple, ochre-glowing buildings; gardens of neatly clipped hedges framing gravel paths – you could almost be in Umbria. The interior is elegant and restrained. 🕲 *Estrada de Monserrate • 21 929 01 70 • www.quintadacapela.com • €€€€*

9 Fortaleza do Guincho
Housed in an old fortress, on a cliff by Guincho beach, this hotel makes good use of the romantic potential of its windswept location, vaulted rooms and grand staircases. Best of all are the junior suites, with arcaded terraces facing the Atlantic. The restaurant has one Michelin star. 🕲 *Estrada do Guincho, Cascais • 21 487 04 91 • www. guinchotel.pt • €€€€€*

10 Saboia
Among Estoril's mid-price hotels, this one has the advantage that all its rooms have balconies – most, but not all, have sea views. Rooms are plain but comfortable. The location is handy for access to both Cascais and Estoril, and the train station is short but steep walk away. 🕲 *Rua do Belmonte 1, Monte Estoril • 21 468 02 02 • www. hotelsaboia.com • €€*

Price Categories

For a standard, double room per night (with breakfast if included), taxes and extra charges.

€	under €50
€€	€50–100
€€€	€100–€175
€€€€	€175–€250
€€€€€	over €250

Avenida Parque

Streetsmart

🔟 Self-catering, Family and Camping

VIP Eden
Housed in what was the grand Art-Deco Eden theatre, overlooking Restauradores, the VIP Eden is Lisbon's most central and well-equipped aparthotel. The rooftop pool has great views over the heart of the city. ® Praça dos Restauradores 24 • Map L2 • 21 321 66 00 • www.viphotels.com • €€€

Tivoli Jardim
Centrally located, just behind the main Tivoli (see p112), reasonably priced and with a round swimming pool, this is a good option for families – albeit one that is also popular with business people. ® Rua Júlio César Machado 7–9 • Map F3 • 21 359 10 00 • www. tivolihotels.com • €€€

Avenida Parque
Just off Parque Eduardo VII (see p91), this hotel offers good value and a practical location. Most rooms overlook the park; some have balconies. ® Avenida Sidónio Pais 6 • Map F2 • 21 353 21 81 • www. avenidaparquehotel.com • €€

Roma
A pensão residencial, the Roma has 25 rooms and 12 small apartments equipped with kitchen-ettes. It's a basic place, but sound and clean, and the location is great, just around the corner from

the Elevador da Glória (see p73). The apartments are on the third and fourth floors of the building; there is no lift. ® Travessa da Glória 22A • Map K2 • 21 346 05 57 • www. residenciaroma.com • €€

Clarion Suites
This well-equipped mid-range hotel is to be found near the Marquês de Pombal roundabout. Standard suites are small and have kitchenettes. More swish penthouse suites are also available. ® Rua Rodrigo da Fonseca 44 • Map F3 • 21 004 66 00 • www.choicehotels europe.com • €€€

Real Residência
Comprising 22 suites and two studios, all with kitchenettes, this suite hotel stands just across the street from the Gulbenkian Museum (see pp24–5), while Parque Eduardo VII is a few blocks away. Guests have access to the health club at sister hotel the Real Palácio (see p112), which is located a bit farther away. ® Rua Ramalho Ortigão 41 • Map F1 • 21 382 29 00 • www. hoteisreal.com • €€€

Altis Suites
This aparthotel is part of the Portuguese Altis chain and immediately adjacent to the larger Altis hotel (see p112). That means it comes with all amenities, along with a central location and a

family-oriented staff. ® Rua Castilho 13 • Map F3 • 21 319 14 00 • www. altishotels.com • €€€

Lisboa Camping
Lisbon's main camp-site is located in the Monsanto park (see p83), immediately west of the centre. Well equipped in practical as well as leisure terms, it can get crowded in the summer, particularly at weekends. Those who prefer a solid roof over their heads can rent a bungalow. ® Estrada Circunvalação • Map B3 • 21 762 82 00 • www. lisboacamping.com • €

Camping Orbitur, Guincho
Attractively located among umbrella pines behind the dunes of Guincho beach, this campsite is popular with surfers. Among its facilities is a tennis court. Bungalows are available. ® Estrada da Areia, Cascais • 21 487 04 50 • www.orbitur.pt • €

Camping Orbitur, Costa da Caparica
Situated near the northern end of the Caparica coast, this campsite set among pines is just 200 m (220 yards) from the beach. Many lisboetas have semi-permanent set ups here, and it can get pretty crowded in the summer. ® Avda Afonso de Albuquerque, Quinta S António • 21 290 13 66 • www.orbitur.pt • €

For tips on things to do with children See pp50–51

General Index

General Index

Acknowledgements

The Author

Tomas Tranæus is a travel writer, translator and photographer based in Lisbon and Madrid. He has contributed to *Eyewitness Portugal* and *Lisbon*, and to the *Time Out* guide to Lisbon. He also writes for Swedish publications.

The author would like to thank the editor for his cool grip and his courteous ways, and the main photographer for his amiable company.

Special thanks for his invaluable assistance to Carlos Oliveira, and to his colleagues at the Portuguese National Tourist Office, London, and the Lisbon Tourist Association, Lisbon.

Produced by Coppermill Books, 55 Salop Road London E17 7HS
Editorial Director Chris Barstow
Designer Ian Midson
Copy Editors Jane Oliver-Jedrzejak, Charles Phillips & Michael Wright
Proofreader Antony Mason
Indexer Hilary Bird
Main Photographer Antony Souter
Additional Photography Paul Bernhardt, Mark Harding, Linda Whitwam, Peter Wilson
Illustrator Chapel Design & Marketing
Maps Mapping Ideas

FOR DORLING KINDERSLEY
Publisher Douglas Amrine
Publishing Manager Fay Franklin
Design Managers Sunita Gahir, Mabel Chan
Senior Cartographic Editor Casper Morris
DTP Designer Natasha Lu
Production Controller Rita Sinha

Design and Editorial Assistance

Emma Anacootee, Tessa Bindloss, Rhiannon Furbear, Quadrum Solutions

Picture Credits

Placement Key: t-top; tl-top left; tlc-top left centre; tc-top centre; tr-top right; cla-centre left above; ca-centre above; cra-centre right above; cl-centre left; c-centre; cr-centre right; clb-centre left below; cb-centre below; crb-centre right below; bl-bottom left, b-bottom; bc-bottom centre; bcl-bottom centre left; br-bottom right; d-detail.
Every effort has been made to trace the copyright holders and we apologize in advance for any unintentional omissions. We would be pleased to insert the appropriate acknowledgments in any subsequent edition of this publication.

The publishers would like to thank the following individuals, companies and picture libraries for their kind permission to reproduce their photographs.

ALAMY IMAGES: James Nesterwitz 62tr; IMAGES OF PORTUGAL: José Manuel 26tl; António Sacchetti 26bl; Bernardo Amaral 49tr; Joaquim Lobo 49br LUXFRAGIL: 42t MUSEU CALOUSTE GULBENKIAN, LISBON: 25tl MUSEU DA CIDADE, LISBON: 31tl TOMAS TRANÆUS: 38tr, 38bl, 46tr, 51tr, 59cr, 60tl, 60tr, 61tl, 67tl, 67tr, 68tl, 68tc, 68tr, 74tl, 74tr, 75tr, 76tr, 85tl, 86tl, 87tl, 88tl, 88tr, 89tl, 94tr, 95tl, 107tl, 107tr, 109tl, 110tr, 111tl, 111tr, 112tl,112tr, 113tl, 114tl, 115tl, 116tr

All other images are © Dorling Kindersley. For further information see *www.dkimages.com*

Phrase Book

In an Emergency

Help!	**Socorro!**	soo-koh-roo
Stop!	**Páre!**	pahr'
Call a doctor!	**Chame um médico!**	shahm' ooñ meh-dee-koo
Call an ambulance!	**Chame uma ambulância!**	shahm' oo-muh añ-boo-lañ-see-uh
Call the police!	**Chame a polícia!**	shahm' uh poo-lee-see-uh
Call the fire brigade!	**Chame os bombeiros!**	shahm' oosh bom-bay-roosh

Communication Essentials

Yes	**Sim**	seeñ
No	**Não**	nowñ
Please	**Por favor/ Faz favor**	poor fuh-vor/ fash fuh-vor
Thank you	**Obrigado/da**	o-bree-gah-doo/duh
Excuse me	**Desculpe**	dish-koolp'
Hello	**Olá**	oh-lah
Goodbye	**Adeus**	a-deh-oosh
Yesterday	**Ontem**	oñ-tayñ
Today	**Hoje**	ohj'
Tomorrow	**Amanhã**	ah-mañ-yañ
Here	**Aqui**	uh-kee
There	**Ali**	uh-lee
What?	**O quê?**	oo keh
Which?	**Qual?**	kwahl'
When?	**Quando?**	kwañ-doo
Why?	**Porquê?**	poor-keh
Where?	**Onde?**	oñd'

Useful Phrases

How are you?	**Como está?**	koh-moo shtah
Very well, thank you	**Bem, obrigado/da.**	bayñ o-bree-gah-doo/duh
Where is/are …?	**Onde está/estão …?**	oñd' shtah/ shtowñ
How far is it to …?	**A que distância fica … ?**	uh kee dish-tañ-see-uh fee-kuh
Which way to …?	**Como se vai para … ?**	koh-moo seh vy puh-ruh
Do you speak English?	**Fala inglês?**	fah-luh eeñ-glehsh
I don't understand	**Não compreendo**	nowñ kom-pree-eñ-doo
Could you speak more slowly please?	**Pode falar mais devagar por favor?**	pohd' fuh-lar mysh d'-va-gar poor fuh-vor
I'm sorry	**Desculpe**	dish-koolp'

Useful Words

big	**grande**	grañd'
small	**pequeno**	pe-keh-noo
hot	**quente**	keñt'
cold	**frio**	free-oo
good	**bom**	boñ
bad	**mau**	mah-oo
open	**aberto**	a-behr-too
closed	**fechado**	fe-shah-doo
left	**esquerda**	shkehr-duh
right	**direita**	dee-ray-tuh
straight on	**em frente**	ayñ freñt'
near	**perto**	pehr-too
far	**longe**	loñj'
up	**para cima**	pur-ruh see-muh
down	**para baixo**	pur-ruh buy-shoo
early	**cedo**	seh-doo
late	**tarde**	tard'

entrance	**entrada**	eñ-trah-duh
exit	**saída**	sa-ee-duh
toilets	**casa de banho**	kah-zuh d' bañ-yoo
more	**mais**	mysh
less	**menos**	meh-noosh

Shopping

How much does this cost?	**Quanto custa isto?**	kwañ-too koosh-tuh eesh-too
I would like …	**Queria …**	kree-uh
I'm just looking	**Estou só a ver obrigado/a**	shtoh soh uh vehr o-bree-gah-doo/uh
Do you take credit cards?	**Aceita cartões de crédito?**	uh-say-tuh kar-toinsh de kreh-dee-too
What time do you open?	**A que horas abre?**	uh kee oh-rash ah-bre
What time do you close?	**A que horas fecha?**	uh kee oh-rash fay-shuh
This/that one	**Este/Esse**	ehst'/ehss'
expensive	**caro**	kah-roo
cheap	**barato**	buh-rah-too
size	**tamanho**	ta-man-yoo
white	**branco**	brañ-koo
black	**preto**	preh-too
red	**vermelho**	ver-mehl-yoo
yellow	**amarelo**	uh-mah-reh-loo
green	**verde**	vehrd'
blue	**azul**	uh-zool'
bakery	**padaria**	pah-duh-ree-uh
bank	**banco**	bañ-koo
bookshop	**livraria**	lee-vruh-ree-uh
cake shop	**pastelaria**	pash-te-luh-ree-uh
chemist	**farmácia**	far-mah-see-uh
market	**mercado**	mehr-kah-doo
newsagent	**kiosque**	kee-yohsk'
post office	**correios**	koo-ray-oosh

Sightseeing

cathedral	**sé**	seh
church	**igreja**	ee-gray-juh
garden	**jardim**	jar-deeñ
library	**biblioteca**	bee-blee-oo-teh-kuh
museum	**museu**	moo-zeh-oo
tourist information office	**posto de turismo**	posh-too d' too-reesh-moo
bus station	**estação de autocarros**	shta-sowñ d' oh-too-kah-roosh
railway station	**estação de comboios**	shta-sowñ d' koñ-boy-oosh

Staying in a Hotel

Do you have a vacant room?	**Tem um quarto livre?**	tayñ ooñ kwar-too leev'
room with a bath	**um quarto com casa de banho**	ooñ kwar-too koñ kah-zuh d' bañ-yoo
shower	**duche**	doosh
single room	**quarto individual**	kwar-too een-dee-vee-doo-ahl'
double room	**quarto de casal**	kwar-too d' kah-zahl'
twin room	**quarto com duas camas**	kwar-too koñ doo-ash kah-mash
I have a reservation	**Tenho um quarto reservado**	tayñ-yoo ooñ kwar-too-re-ser-vah-doo

Eating Out

Have you got a table for ..?	Tem uma mesa para ... ?	tayñ oo-muh meh-zuh puh-ruh
I want to reserve a table	Quero reservar uma mesa	keh-roo re-zehr-var o-muh meh-zuh
The bill please	A conta por favor/ faz favor	uh kohn-tuh poor fuh-vor/ fash fuh-vor
I am a vegetarian	Sou vegetariano/a	Soh ve-je-tuh-ree-ah-noo/uh
the menu	a lista	uh leesh-tuh
wine list	a lista de vinhos	uh leesh-tuh de veeñ-yoosh
glass	um copo	ooñ koh-poo
bottle	uma garrafa	oo-muh guh-rah-fuh
knife	uma faca	oo-muh fah-kuh
fork	um garfo	ooñ gar-foo
spoon	uma colher	oo-muh kool-yair
plate	um prato	ooñ prah-too
breakfast	pequeno-almoço	pe-keh-noo-ahl-moh-soo
lunch	almoço	ahl-moh-soo
dinner	jantar	jan-tar
starter	entrada	eñ-trah-duh
main course	prato principal	prah-too prin-see-pahl'
dessert	sobremesa	soh-bre-meh-zuh
rare	mal passado	mahl' puh-sah-doo
medium	médio	meh-dee-oo
well done	bem passado	bayñ puh-sah-doo

Menu Decoder

açorda	uh-sor-duh	bread-based stew
açúcar	uh-soo-kar	sugar
água mineral	ah-gwuh mee-ne-rahl'	mineral water
(com gás)	koñ gas	sparkling
(sem gás)	sayñ gas	still
alho	al-yoo	garlic
amêijoas	uh-may-joo-ash	clams
arroz	uh-rohsh	rice
atum	uh-tooñ	tuna
azeitonas	uh-zay-toh-nash	olives
bacalhau	buh-kuh-lyow	dried, salted cod
batatas	buh-tah-tash	potatoes
batatas fritas	buh-tah-tash free-tash	french fries
bica	bee-kuh	espresso
bife	beef	steak
bolo	boh-loo	cake
borrego	boo-reh-goo	lamb
café	kuh-feh	coffee
camarões	kuh-muh-roysh	large prawns
caranguejo	kuh-rañ-gay-joo	crab
carne	karn'	meat
cebola	se-boh-luh	onion
cerveja	sehr-vay-juh	beer
chouriço	shoh-ree-soo	red, spicy sausage
cogumelos	koo-goo-meh-loosh	mus
fiambre	fee-añbr'	ham
fígado	fee-guh-doo	liver
frango	frañ-goo	chicken
frito	free-too	fried
fruta	froo-tuh	fruit
gambas	gam-bash	prawns
gelado	je-lah-doo	ice cream
gelo	jeh-loo	ice
grelhado	grel-yah-d	squid
maçã	muh-sañ	apple
manteiga	mañ-tay-guh	butter
mariscos	muh-reesh-koosh	seafood
ostras	osh-trash	oysters

ovos	oh-voosh	eggs
pão	powñ	bread
pastel	pash-tehl'	cake
pato	pah-too	duck
peixe	paysh'	fish
pimenta	pee-meñ-tuh	pepper
polvo	pohl'-voo	octopus
porco	por-coo	pork
queijo	kay-joo	cheese
sal	sahl'	salt
salada	suh-lah-duh	salad
salsichas	sahl-see-shash	sausages
sopa	soh-puh	soup
sumo	soo-moo	juice
tamboril	tañ-boo-ril'	monkfish
tomate	too-maht'	tomato
vinho branco	veeñ-yoo brañ-koo	white wine
vinho tinto	veeñ-yoo teeñ-too	red wine
vitela	vee-teh-luh	veal

Numbers

0	zero	zeh-roo
1	um	ooñ
2	dois	doysh
3	três	tresh
4	quatro	kwa-troo
5	cinco	seeñ-koo
6	seis	saysh
7	sete	set'
8	oito	oy-too
9	nove	nov'
10	dez	desh
11	onze	oñz'
12	doze	doz'
13	treze	trez'
14	catorze	ka-torz'
15	quinze	keeñz'
16	dezasseis	de-zuh-saysh
17	dezassete	de-zuh-set'
18	dezoito	de-zoy-too
19	dezanove	de-zuh-nov'
20	vinte	veent'
21	vinte e um	veen-tee-ooñ
30	trinta	treeñ-tuh
40	quarenta	kwa-reñ-tuh
50	cinquenta	seen-kweñ-tuh
60	sessenta	se-señ-tuh
70	setenta	se-teñ-tuh
80	oitenta	oy-teñ-tuh
90	noventa	noo-veñ-tuh
100	cem	sayñ
101	cento e um	señ-too-ee-ooñ
200	duzentos	doo-zeñ-toosh
300	trezentos	tre-zeñ-toosh
400	quatrocentos	kwa-troo-señ-toosh
500	quinhentos	kee-nyeñ-toosh
700	setecentos	set'-señ-toosh
900	novecentos	nov'-señ-toosh
1,000	mil	meel'

Time

one minute	um minuto	ooñ mee-noo-too
one hour	uma hora	oo-muh oh-ruh
half an hour	meia-hora	may-uh-oh-ruh
Monday	segunda-feira	se-goon-duh-fay-ruh
Tuesday	terça-feira	ter-sa-fay-ruh
Wednesday	quarta-feira	kwar-ta-fay-ruh
Thursday	quinta-feira	keen-ta-fay-ruh
Friday	sexta-feira	say-shta-fay-ruh
Saturday	sábado	sah-ba-doo
Sunday	domingo	doo-meen-goo

Selected Street Index